THROUGH MANY TOILS AND SNARES

The story of a lifetime spent mainly in Africa

Michael Chesterman

To my wife Sylvia

who stuck by me through thick and thin

CONTENTS

EARLY DAYS

The late 19th century 'Scramble for Africa'. You read about it in the history books. King Leopold of the Belgians grabbed that vast area of Africa then known as the Congo, and exploited it mercilessly. Fortunately the colony later became Congo Belge, under the more civilised rule of the Belgian government. Mission stations were established along the banks of the Congo river. One of these, on the equator near what was then called Stanleyville, was Yakusu, managed by the BMS, the Baptist Missionary Society. In 1920 my parents travelled out by sea from Antwerp to Matadi, then by rail to Leopoldville. The final leg of their journey was by river-steamer, 1,000 miles upstream. At last (after 14 days on board) they reached the landing-stage on the river-bank at Yakusu, ready to start work as BMS missionaries. My father a doctor, my mother a teacher.

Yakusu Hospital

Twelve years later in 1932, after furlough (missionary jargon for leave) in UK they repeated the journey

'Crossing the Line' 17 November 1932 on board the Anversville

This time, as they walked down the gang-plank at Yakusu, they were carrying a cot with a 3-months old baby boy inside. Me!

Before long I was writing letters to my two elder brothers and elder sister in England. For example one dated April 1934 said "I will tell you lovely stories about the new Church. The bricks are being burnt. I go down and look at the huge fires and am a little afraid but not much". Actually it wasn't me who wrote the letters, but my Mum, with the pretence that it was me. She and my father had had no choice but to leave their first three children in UK in the care of relatives – a huge sacrifice. In those days the health risks of tropical areas of Africa were considered to be too high to allow missionaries to take their children with them. By the time I was born the rules were relaxed, which explains why I was able to grow up as a toddler with my parents, at Yakusu.

My letter dated January 1935 ended as follows "I still help to build the new church but it will not be finished before I go to England, a place I know nothing about yet. I was just born there and then came here, and here is the place for Michael Paul Chesterman".

Yakusu's 'New' Church

It was this sense of my having my 'roots' at Yakusu which prompted me 52 years later, in 1987, to accept an invitation to attend a thanksgiving service, in that very same Ndako Ya Mungu (House of God) where as a 2-yr old I had picked up a hoe and made bricks with mud. My last 'Yakusu letter', to my brother Frederick in April 1936, struck a prophetic note "some day when you have been made into a doctor..." Sure enough, this later happened.

AT SCHOOL

Back in England, our family home from 1936 until the outbreak of war in 1939 was my birthplace, Bath. My grandfather (on my mother's side) Frederick Spear had been elected ("with acclamation" so the records say) Mayor of Bath in 1917. With his brother he ran a well-known bacon and pork factory in the city centre. Spear's sausages were in high demand. My other (Chesterman) grandfather, a solicitor, had seven sons. They were all marched off to Manvers St Baptist church every Sunday. From the gallery they would look down and smile at the three Spear daughters sitting in the congregation below. My father (Clement) and uncle (Paul) courted and married two of them, Winifred and Daisy. Sadly my uncle Phil was too shy (so they say) to propose to the third Spear sister, Hilda. It's funny the things you remember of your childhood. One of the few memories I have of my time at Alpine Cottage on Beechen Cliff is my sitting on the stone wall at the end of the garden, swinging my legs and looking out over the city spread out below me. I used to look east to the exit of the railway tunnel at Box, several miles away. In those days the express train from London to Bristol was non-stop. If you wanted to get off in Bath you had to sit in the last 3 coaches – slip-coaches they were called. At the right moment, just after coming out of Box tunnel, the guard would pull a lever to uncouple the last 3 coaches, which would then 'freewheel' into Bath Spa station. As a 7-year old boy I would delight in shouting "NOW!" to tip off the guard. Sure enough a gap would open up and widen as the express thundered on, leaving the slip-coaches behind!

In the war years we moved to Little Chalfont in Buckinghamshire, where my father was a partner (GP) in a medical practice. Few memories of that remain, other than that of my ending up as Head Boy of the prep school I attended. According to the Headmaster's 1944 report on me "he has shown an excellent example". After the war we moved to Hampstead, where I attended University College School (UCS). Striking red and black stripes on my new school blazer, and a school motto in Latin – Paulatim- meaning little by little. On my Report for 1948 one of the Form-master's comments was "he remains in his work and manner quite unpredictable". Fortunately the closing comment was that "his pleasant personality and friendly smile can, however, be relied upon". As I took my Higher School Certificate just before I was 17, I had what these days is called a 'Gap Year' to play with, before going up to read Modern Languages at Cambridge. An interesting and unusual opportunity presented itself. Read on!

GAP YEAR

My father's role as a consultant in tropical medicine kept him in touch with counterparts in many places. One of these professional colleagues was Dr Samuel Mueller of the German Institute for Medical Mission, based in Tubingen. Through his good offices it was arranged that I should enrol for a year's study at Tubingen University, staying as a guest in his home. So off I went in September 1949, grateful for the opportunity to be one of the first few British students to attend a German university after the war.

Tubingen University Main Block (the Aula) in 1950

At that time defeated Germany was partitioned into 4 zones of occupation (Besatzungszonen), Tubingen being in the French zone. That explained why the flag flying on local masts was the tricolour, not the schwarz/rot/gold of Germany. The post-war mood of my generation was to re-act strongly against the folly and horrors of war. "Ohne uns" was a typical slogan among students, roughly "Keep us out of it". I remember a popular song, sung with sarcastic humour rather than seriously, "Jetzt werden wir alle entnazifiziert" ("Now we are all being de-nazified"). As I saw it, there was little need for a formal de-nazification process. The mood was for friendship, not enmity. So I felt welcome, as I plunged into my studies. The course for which I enrolled was called 'Germanistik'. It was a curious mix of

German culture, philosophy, music, and even, by my choice, some theology. This was thanks to the reputation of a famous professor, Dr Helmut Thielicke, then lecturing on the Parables (Gleichnisreden) of Jesus. ; 'Entmythologisierung' was his theme. How the Germans love long words! It means de-mythologising, if that leaves you any the wiser. Heavy going, but I did my best to grasp the gist.

The Germans' love of music captured me (and has remained with me ever since). Every Sunday, in addition to the grand old Lutheran hymns sung by the congregation in the mediaeval Stiftskirche, the choir would sing a motet, often a Bach cantata. Shortly after sunrise on Sundays a brass band (Posaunenchor) would climb up to the balcony on the church tower. In the still, crisp coolness the sound of a Bach Chorale, such as "Wie schon leuchtet der Morgenstern", would float across to me, listening at the window of my little room a mile away.

In the Muellers' home the box of dominoes would come out after supper, and it was heads down for an hour for serious business around the table. 12 years later this friendship would result in my being invited to Tanzania – but that of course is another story. My time in Tubingen in 1950 gave me both fluency in German and a flying start when I went up to Cambridge to read Modern Languages.

Tubingen
The Marktplatz and the Rathaus
(Town Hall)

Tubingen
Market Place fountain

UNIVERSITY

My room at Christ's College
was T6, in 3rd Court.

Let's face it – much of my time and energy at Cambridge was spent on the water. Despite that however, I managed to get both a Degree and a Diploma of Education, so it all worked out, shall we say, satisfactorily.   As an oarsman I was not a beginner, having learnt to row at school. So for all 4 years 1950-54 I was in the Christ's College first boat. Two 'blades' hang on the wall in my home as a reminder of success. In the May races of 1952 Christ's 1st boat made 4 bumps. This qualified for the reward of 'winning your oars'. 8 ft long and inscribed with the names of the crew, their weights (I was 12 stone 8 lbs), and the College crest.   Bumps racing is a curious affair. Because the river Cam is so narrow and bendy, you can't race side by side. All crews line up at precisely measured intervals, and all spring into action when the starting-gun fires. They chase each other madly, trying to close the gap and 'bump' (i.e. bump into) the crew in front. If you succeed, next day you start ahead of the crew you bumped. My other blade records that my friend Freddie Bircher and I in 1953 won the University Pairs in a (then) record time of 6.59.

The 1952 Christ's College crew went on to a dramatic disaster in the Thames Challenge Cup at Henley Regatta. Against the University of Pennsylvania we were well in the lead in the Final, as we rowed past the Enclosures, cheered on by the patriotic crowd. 20 strokes from the Finish our No 3 caught a crab, slowing us down. Consternation! The crowd hushed. Our rivals rowed past to take the Cup. Ah well, - some you win, some you lose. That's life.

You can't mistake it. It's Henley Regatta. 1952.
Christ's College leading in the Final of the Thames Cup.

Being adventurous youngsters we then drove overland to Hamburg, in Freddie Bircher's much admired ancient open-top Bentley, to compete in the regatta there on the Binnenalster. We won the Schifffahrtsachter, but sadly we trailed behind in the Senatsachter, because the other crews all blasted off before the starter said Go! At least it was all good fun.

Nearly a Blue - twice !

Two Trial Eights race each other in December each year. Out of the *sixteen* oarsmen, eight go on to race against Oxford in the Boat Race. In 1953 and 1954 I was 'in the running' for a Cambridge Blue, but just missed out both times. Pity.

'The Times' dated 18 Feb 1954 commented that "The crew seems to have been chosen for safety, and one cannot help wondering whether in the circumstances it might not have been better to take a chance on one or two stronger men whose form may sometimes have been erratic. One thinks, in particular, of M. P. Chesterman and F. M. Bircher of Christ's, both of whom are great racers".

Alongside all this my studies progressed. In Year 2 I switched from Modern Languages to Economics. A confusing subject. A fellow-student asked the Professor why every year the exam questions were predictable. "No problem," he replied. "Every year we change the answers!"

MARRIAGE AND FAMILY

1954 was to see my engagement, in Scotland, to Sylvia.

The best thing that ever happened to me was to meet and then marry Sylvia Peake. While studying at Cambridge I was a member of the Robert Hall Society, a group of students with Baptist backgrounds. One of their activities during summer vacation was to go on 'missions' to various places. In 1953 we went off to London, at the invitation of a big Baptist Church there, the West Ham Central Mission. They kindly organised a group of their own young people to join us, as these 'toffs' from Cambridge would need help and guidance in coming to terms with the culture of the East End! One of the West Ham team was Sylvia Peake, then studying Physical Education at Dartford College. We became engaged, and later were married at West Ham Central Mission on 9 April 1955.

Henley-on-Thames became our first home after we married. At first we lived in a rented flat in the Fair Mile. I remember I was then so fit that I could easily leap up the stairs to the third floor. Our first child, Graham, was born in the local hospital in 1956, so in addition to my sweaty rowing kit my wife had nappies to wash. Before long we moved a few miles up the road to the first home of our own, in the tiny village of Cookley Green. We called our house 'Morven', after the name of the mountain in Scotland on the summit of which I had proposed. Our second son Ian was born there (the house, not the mountain) in September 1957.

At this time I was serving, by compulsion rather than choice, in the Royal Air Force – "2733058 Flying Officer Chesterman, Sir ", if my memory is correct. (They say a serviceman never forgets his number, but I'm not so sure.) Instead of doing 2 years National Service, I chose the option of a 3 year Short Service Commission, one advantage of this being entitlement to a marriage allowance. 'Flying Officers' don't necessarily fly. It's the rank you go up to when you get promotion from one very thin single blue stripe on your sleeve to a thicker one. I was in the Education Branch, and taught rank-and-file airmen basic subjects such as English and Current affairs. Stationed at RAF Benson, I found myself (surprise, surprise!) being Captain of the RAF Rowing Club, out on the river at Wallingford in all weathers, and competing in regattas at home and abroad. It was a tough discipline. Eventually I handed over the job, in favour of a quiet life.

NIGERIA

A letter to me dated 26th November 1957 read

"Sir. I am commanded by the Air Council to convey to you their thanks for the services which you have rendered to the Royal Air Force. I am, Sir, your obedient servant, xxx".

Well, that was nice, but now what? I was 25, married, with two young sons, (one a toddler, the other a baby). It had to be Africa. But where in Africa? The answer turned out to be Nigeria. 'Assistant Master on the staff of C.M.S. Grammar School, Lagos, w.e.f. January 1958', said the Contract... 'First or Tourist Class passage provided free both ways'.

We duly boarded the M.V, Apapa (Elder Dempster Lines) at Liverpool, for the long (10 days was it?) voyage by sea to Lagos. Tourist Class. Separate meal times for children. First stop Bathurst, capital of Gambia. Brief excursion to 'see the sights'. Smelly open sewers running down the side of the streets. Colourful market. Very hot and steamy. Result – our young son Graham got glandular fever. Not the best start for us! Careful nursing needed to ensure his recovery.

CMS Grammar School Lagos was an old-established mission institution. The School Song, entitled 'Up! And On!' reflects its colonial origin and curious ethos. I can't help but quote the Chorus for you...

> 'Up boys! Truest fame lies in high endeavour.
> Play the game! Keep the flame burning brightly ever!

The rhetoric escalates to a triumphant (and politically correct) final verse:

> Africa will surely rise. Fail we not in high emprise,
> Hidden here the secret lies, UP! and ON!'

Our arrival coincided with the move of the school to a new site on the outskirts of Lagos.

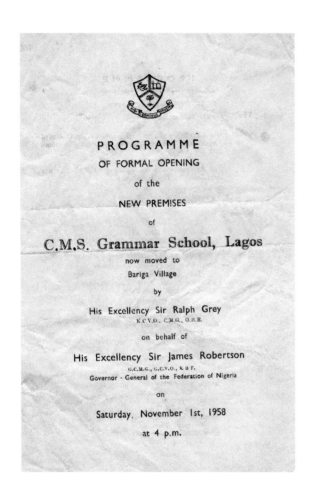

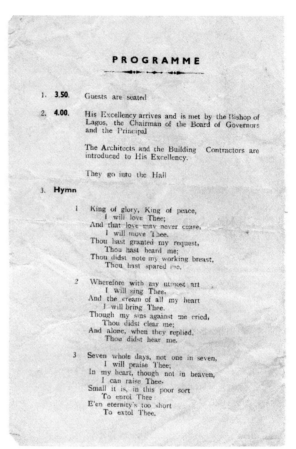

'Cross the Carter Bridge, turn off to the little village of Bariga, and be greeted by the Principal, Canon Adelaja'. A remarkable person.

Shortly after moving in to our modest staff bungalow we heard gunshots at sunset. "What's that?" we asked our neighbour. "Oh, don't worry. It's Canon Adelaja, firing off a few shots to scare away the evil spirits". Another memory (it's funny what sticks in your mind, isn't it?) is of playing Scrabble at home in the evenings with staff colleagues. One of them, when stuck with a tile he didn't want, surreptitiously managed to drop it down the inside of his trousers, onto the floor, where we would find it when the game was over.

Visit of the Minister of Education

After a year, for various reasons, we saw fit to give notice. A fresh challenge lay ahead of us, not far away as it turned out, as a Lecturer in the Teacher Training College at Winneba, in Ghana. Just time for Christmas 1958 back in UK with family, and then off to Winneba.

GHANA

You remember the dramatic pictures of the end of the Iraqi war – the towering statue of President Saddam being toppled from its pedestal? Well, a similar thing happened previously in Ghana, when the shine of Independence had worn off a bit and the realities of a virtual dictatorship were being felt. On the base of the pedestal in Accra, on which stood the imposing statue of Kwame Nkrumah, the caption read 'Seek ye first the political kingdom.' Eventually the statue was toppled, but that was after my time in Ghana, which started at Winneba in February 1959. My job at the Teacher Training College included two roles – classroom teaching, and also being Warden of a Students Hostel. I was assigned to run Hall Five. My wife and I soon developed a good working relationship with the students, and they responded by excelling in their studies, extra-curricular activities, and sport.

Winneba is on the coast of the Atlantic. One big problem of the Gold Coast (as Ghana was known in colonial times) was the lack of deep-water harbours. Winneba was a 'surfing' port. Ships lay at anchor off-shore, heaving up and down in the swell. Small surf-boats had to paddle out to them through the breakers. Cargo was then unloaded precariously. Timing is crucial – the load has to be released when the ship and the surfboat are both moving up, or down, *together*. Tricky. There was one advantage to local residents like us of the big difference in levels of the tide. The swimming-pool on the beach drained and filled daily. For our two very young boys, Graham and Ian, life at the seaside was fun. Then along came our third son, born in Winneba Hospital in 1961. Official English name was Colin, but to the locals he was Kofi Mensah (3rd son, born on a Friday).

My teaching duties included Current Affairs. To give students an insight into what the 'Cold War' was all about I invited the Ambassadors of USA and the Soviet Union (as then was) to give talks. Interesting! The internal politics of Ghana at that time needed to be treated vey diplomatically, because of the personality cult built up around the President.

Wherever his motorised cavalcade passed, cheering crowds at the roadside chanted "Osagyefo, Akwaaba" – meaning "Saviour! Welcome!"

During the holidays we fitted in visits to the old slave forts further along the coast – grim reminders of the curse of slavery. It was with considerable regret that in April 1961 we eventually said Goodbye to Ghana.

Hall 5 students at Winneba Training College 1959

THE GERMAN CONNECTION

The opening sentence of this book referred to the Scramble for Africa. That took place at the Berlin Conference of 1884, when European powers grabbed swathes of Africa as colonies. Germany got two big slices, one being Deutsch OstAfrika, (later renamed Tanganyika when Germany lost it at the end of the Great War). In the northeast (Tanga Province) lay the area of the Usambara mountains. The high altitude here means that the climate is temperate rather than tropical. No surprise therefore that many German settlers moved in. German Lutheran missionaries too. In their mission stations they set up churches, schools, hospitals. At Vuga, half-way up the steep and narrow Soni Pass from the plains to the plateau, they established a printing press. And it was here, at Vuga Press, that the manager in 1961 was Tulo Mueller.

Mueller? That name rings a bell (see a previous chapter in this book). It was in the home of Tulo's parents, Dr and Mrs Samuel Mueller, that I spent my Gap year as a student in Germany in 1950. Tulo and I had then become good friends. Naturally our ways had parted – mine to W. Africa and his to E. Africa. When he and his father got to hear in 1961 that I was out of a job and looking for another one, they came up with a startling proposition. Would I be interested in becoming Headmaster of a new secondary school being set up at Magamba, near Lushoto in the Usambaras? Interested? I responded at once, positively.

Of course there had to be interviews and discussions. That involved my going to Germany, to the offices in Bielefeld of the Bethel Mission. They would be my official 'sending agency', sponsoring and supporting me for missionary service in Tanganyika under the management of the Usambara-Digo Lutheran Church. Incidentally, (and here I digress for a moment), the Bethel Mission was founded by the legendary Pastor Bodelschwingh in Victorian times (1867) to care for people suffering from epilepsy and mental illness. Subsequently the Mission opened up similar ministry abroad in Tanganyika, caring for the disabled. (One such institution, a School for the Blind, was situated not far from Magamba).

So it was that in August 1961 I spent a month at the Bethel Mission HQ, prior to our return later in the year to Africa once again, as a family, with 3 young boys. It turned out to be a period of rewarding fulfilment and agonising frustration. It is hardly surprising that in the light of the events described I chose 'Through many toils and snares' as the title of this book. To see why, simply read on!

TANZANIA

MAGAMBA

Just getting there is an adventure in itself. Scenic drive, you could call it. From the coast at Tanga through the sisal plantations to the turn-off at Mombo, at the foot of the escarpment, it's easy going. Then for an hour it's low gear and a succession of sharp hairpin bends, as you wind up the pass to Soni Falls and beyond to reach the bustling market town of Lushoto. This is the boma – the District headquarters, with a police-station, bank, post-office, even a hotel! Keep going for another 4 miles uphill, with the big eucalyptus trees on the verges protecting you from the steep drop down into the valley below. Among the banana trees a cluster of simple huts with tin roofs tells you that you have reached Magamba village. Carry on for a mile or so round the bend, and a strange sight presents itself as you look left. On the terraced hill-side is a relic from colonial times – a set of buildings which was once the Magamba Country Club.

Country Club? Up here in the dense forest? Yes, strange but true! The cool climate of the Usambara mountain-range was a magnet for expatriate staff working in hot and dusty places elsewhere in Tanganyika. Also it attracted a substantial number of settlers, at first German and then British, who built retirement homes beside the trout streams. A bit like the hill-stations in India, where the empire-builders spent their leave and had afternoon tea on the lawn? Here at Magamba there was not only a Country Club, with a bar and guest-rooms, but a 9-hole Golf Course, just a bit further down the road, where the landscape opened up to give magnificent views on all sides. And – can you believe it – this was the site of the new secondary school of which I was to be Headmaster.

Our new home was in a small clearing on the edge of the forest – so close that we could watch the black and white colobus monkeys swinging from the branches.

As the construction of the new school was in its early stages, school activities were on an improvised basis in the country club premises. Enrolment in 1961 was 35 in Form 1, and doubled with a new Form 1 intake in Jan 1962.

MPC   Herman   Kolbjorn   Bill
       Shelukindo Riiser   Robbins

The founder-Headmaster was a Norwegian missionary Kolbjorn Riiser, from whom I took over in April 1962. In my Annual Report for 1962 I paid tribute to him: "The present character of the school derives largely from his influence and the standards and traditions which he established". So I took over with a flying start.

One of these traditions was self-help. This filtered down from the newly elected President of Tanganyika, Mwalimu (Teacher) Dr Julius Nyerere. His slogan was 'Harambee' – let's all pull together. Regardless of rank or status. Accordingly, I piled the boys into the school lorry, and off we went deep into the forest, where tall trees had been felled to provide poles for electricity supply on the new site at the golf course. With harness and ropes we toiled to lug these heavy tree-trunks to the roadside, singing 'Harambee' as we went.

Before long the new classroom block was ready for us to move in. The design was simple yet spectacular – a long frontage, in a shallow V formation with two swept-back wings, on level ground above the gentle slope down to the access road. Stylish dormitories and staff housing dotted about where the golfing greens had once been - Assembly/Dining Hall to follow later at the central V

OPENING CEREMONY OF THE NEW BUILDING Saturday February 9th 1963
by The Hon. S. N. Eliufoo M.P. Minister for Education.

Every Saturday morning after breakfast there was Headmaster's Inspection. This was conducted with military precision – a parade. All boys in smart uniform, led by Prefects. A proper march-past, with 'Eyes right' and a salute. A bit old-fashioned it may seem, by today's standards, but the boys took a pride in it and held their heads high.

In June (1962) the whole school went to Tanga for a week – a major expedition. Visits were made to the Harbour, Airport, Hospital, railway, Town hall, Police station, law court, a ship, the cinema, and the beach. This took the boys out of a severely limited rural home environment (e.g. cattle herding, wattle-bark, and bananas) into the wider world of industry, business, machinery, and so on – educationally very valuable. I remember how one enterprising pupil in Form 2 took us all by surprise. Erasto Mpemba secretly at night used the freezer in the school Science Laboratory to manufacture home-made ice-cream, for his classmates to enjoy. In the process he noted that his warm milk and water froze quicker than a cold milk/water mix. "Strange" he thought "Why is that?" This baffling discovery (Hot water freezes into a solid more rapidly from a heated state than from room temperature) became known internationally as the Mpemba Paradox. It was the subject of a Prize competition in 2013 organised by the Royal Society of Chemistry, no less! My wife and I were invited by the RSC to attend the Prize Giving Ceremony at Burlington House in Piccadilly. There we met Erasto again – 50 years on! A Prize was awarded, but the mystery remains.

At the risk of blowing my own trumpet, allow me to quote here from the Ministry of Education Chief Inspector's remarks under the heading 'General'. 'The school is well organised and boys are kept profitably busy both inside and outside the classroom. The tone of the school is good. Staff and pupils work harmoniously. There is order and attention to detail. A promising start'.

So far so good. But there was trouble brewing, way above my head, in the affairs of U.D.L.C. – the Usambara-Digo Lutheran Church. U.D.L.C. was the 'managing agency' of several institutions, including Magamba Secondary School, the Trade School, Bumbuli

Hospital, the Vuga Press, and so on. Not surprisingly a lot of expensive building work was going on in these places. The programme was under the control of an American missionary administrator in the central U.D.L.C. office. His bright idea was to 'pool' in one kitty all grants and funds available from various sources, and pay the builder out of this kitty as the various bills came in. On record is a letter from him to colleagues, dated 14 November 1962, with a startling admission: "If we can still get hold of the 150,000 (shillings) due from Government for Magamba, then our situation is alright...but if we can't get hold of that money, then we're in trouble." In the event, I made sure he didn't get that money (and he did soon end up in trouble, being sent back to the USA). The incident was later mentioned in an article in the Economist, dated 15 June 1963, entitled 'Tanganyika -Turbulent Priests', with a favourable reference to ' the British headmaster who had stuck to it that funds for education should be spent on education' .

The U.D.L.C., however, had at this time another, bigger, problem, with its internal affairs in disarray, to put it mildly. The background is somewhat complicated. On 9 August 1961 a special Synod of U.D.L.C. convened 'to consider introducing episcopacy leadership,... and if so agreed, to elect a Bishop'. Well, it was so agreed, and on 4 February 1962 a long-serving (30+ years) German missionary pastor Heinrich Waltenberg was consecrated as Bishop. Sadly it wasn't long before, as the documents record, 'widespread dissatisfaction' surfaced. There were concerns about 'unconstitutional procedures' in the election process. There was a feeling that the church authorities had 'jumped the gun' over ratification. There was now clear evidence of schism. On 15 Dec 1962 a new 'countersynod' constituted itself and elected new leadership under a President. On 28 December what you might call the regular Synod of U.D.L.C. convened, composed almost entirely of followers of Bishop Waltenberg. This left a situation of two rival groups/churches confronting each other directly. I shall never forget (I have it recorded on 8mm cine-film) the long procession of the anti-Bishop faction winding its way on foot through the campus at Magamba with banners of protest held aloft ('Waltenberg ni sumu' – 'Waltenberg is poison'). This public disorder called for action by the civil authorities. But what action?

At this point the Minister of Home Affairs in the Government, no less, took the initiative. The Hon Oscar Kambona M.P. summoned the two rival groups in the U.D.L.C. to attend a meeting, chaired by him, for purposes of arbitration. This reflected African culture, whereby disputes in the village are settled by the chief and the elders sitting down together in the shade of the mango tree and talking things through. In this instance the 'mango tree' was to be the shady grounds of the Presidential Lodge just outside Lushoto. Accordingly on 3rd January 1963 all parties to the dispute filed in through the imposing iron gates and took their place, with police in attendance. I was just one of the crowd. The outcome was a diplomatic compromise. Mr Kambona ruled that the incumbent holders of office in the divided U.D.L.C. should step down and be replaced by a temporary committee, consisting of 8 from the Bishop's 'side' and 8 from the other side. There were thus to be no immediate losers or winners. It turned out to be an uneasy alliance. Strict partisan loyalty prevented the 'Committee of 16' from making any substantial progress when it met in February. Stalemate. Fortunately in April a new and smaller (6-man) U.D.L.C. Executive Committee took over. There was every indication that matters were progressing satisfactorily.

Then came the **bombshell.** On 7th May I was summoned urgently to the boma in Lushoto. Without any explanation an official handed me a Form 25B. It was addressed to me and was short and to the point – 'Take notice that you are a prohibited immigrant...under Section 3 of the Immigration Ordinance...and that this declaration has been confirmed by the Minister for Home Affairs... **You are hereby ordered to leave Tanganyika within 25 days,** i.e. by 31/5/63'. Wow! What is more, I was not the only missionary to get this treatment. It applied also to my American friend and colleague Dr Tom Seward (Education Secretary) and my German friend Fritz Lamparter (Manager of the Vuga Press). Protests were lodged, (including one from me); requesting Government to reconsider what was seen as drastic action, but to no avail. Unofficial word related that Bishop Waltenberg was also required to leave and return to Germany - which he did. This could be seen as a kind of trade-off – no winners. So, we (my wife and I and our three young boys) had no choice but to pack up and leave.

The Immigration Regulations, 1957
Regulation ~~34(2)~~ 34(3)

Nº 101

NOTICE TO PROHIBITED IMMIGRANT

To: Mr. Michael Chesterman

Take notice that you are a prohibited immigrant by virtue of the fact that I have declared you to be an undersirable immigrant under paragraph (f) of the definition of prohibited immigrant contained in Section 3 of the Immigration Ordinance, and that my declaration aforesaid has been confirmed by the ~~Governor in Council~~. MINISTER – HOME AFFAIRS.

*(a) You are hereby ordered to leave Tanganyika within 26 Days ie 31/5/63 days by the first available means

*(b) ~~You are hereby ordered to remain on board and to leave Tanganyika by the ship/aircraft on which you arrived at Tanganyika.~~

Dated this........................day of.............................19....

✗ as amended by Ord 58/1961.

*Delete words which do not apply.

Received : MP. Chesterman

J. M. Malchie
Principal Immigration Officer

. On the day of our departure there was an earth tremor, just as the Magamba schoolboys lining the drive were waving goodbye to us. Their immediate reaction was to scatter in alarm. "You are leaving us. God is angry". 46 years later we were invited back to Magamba. But that's another story.

Turbulent Priests

FROM A CORRESPONDENT

FOUR Lutheran missionaries have been expelled from Tanganyika. The only official explanation for this has come from the local area commissioner responsible for the expulsions. He said that the continued stay of the missionaries was " not conducive to peace and good order." It is not an informative explanation : perhaps this is so because the whole explanation is long and complex and goes back, even, to the book of Genesis.

But, for the sake of starting somewhere, take the German missionary, the Reverend Heinrich Waltenberg, who served for many years in Usumbara-Digo, a mountainous area north-east of Tanga. His Lutheran flock numbers 35,000 (it is still there, although Mr Waltenberg is not) and, until two years ago, was a contented flock. Then Mr Waltenberg, as president of the local church, called a synod at which he suggested putting a bishop rather than a president at the head of the church. A bishop would have greater powers.

Many of his followers opposed this change (although their fellow-Lutherans in northern Tanganyika had accepted a similar change) and they pointed to the constitutional provision that the church should wait one year before ratifying it. Even so, Mr Waltenberg became bishop six months after the synod. Then the trouble started. First, the educational secretary, Mr Seward, an American, joined forces with the British headmaster of the church secondary school at Magamba in opposition to the new bishop's educational policy. Then the constitutional squabble went up to the Lutheran world federation. It was sent back to Tanganyika, where the all-Tanganyikan federation of Lutheran churches despatched an investigating committee to the mountains.

On its return, the committee suggested another synod meeting. At this second council, a Tanganyikan priest, Mr Mwanga, was elected president. Mr Waltenberg refused to accept this and the federation appealed to the Tanganyikan government for mediation.

Mr Oscar Kambona, who was then minister of home affairs, took a powerful party up to the mountains. Here ends the recital of known facts ; what follows is partly conjecture. Mr Waltenberg, who may or may not be a bishop, apparently decided to leave the country. The area commissioner then said that Mr Seward and the British headmaster (who had stuck to it that funds for education should be spent on education) and two other missionaries (both of them opponents of Mr Waltenberg) had to leave by May 31st. Since an American missionary who had defended Mr Waltenberg had been withdrawn earlier, this seemed to be a decision to keep the peace by expelling both sides. Dar-es-Salaam took some days to endorse the expulsions ; now it is claimed in Tanganyika that those who left are not bitter and even that the local church is the stronger for it all.

15 June 1963. 'Economist'

WOULD YOU BELIEVE IT?

What do you do if you are a Cambridge graduate, married man with three young children, have unexpectedly lost the good job you had overseas in Tanzania, have returned to UK in mid-summer 1963, are living temporarily with your parents in London, and need to find a teaching post in September? Answer – you phone the Cambridge University Appointments Board and request an interview.

"Ah, take a seat Mr Chesterman. So you are looking for a Modern Languages teaching post? Thanks for sending me your c.v. – very interesting. Somewhat unusual, I must say. One obvious snag is that you haven't got any previous experience of teaching French and German. But we will see what we can do."

Just at that moment the telephone on his desk rang.

"Excuse me – do you mind if I take this incoming call?"

"Go ahead" I said.

I could of course only hear his side of the conversation.

"Ah, Mr Bruce-Lockhart, how can I help you?"

Long pause. He then cupped his hand over the receiver, turned to me, and said "*Would you believe it?* It's the Headmaster of Gresham's School. He's just been let down by the sudden withdrawal of an applicant for the September vacancy in the Modern Languages Dep't. Are you interested?"

I nearly fell off my chair! "Of course" I said. He turned back to the receiver

"As it happens, I have a candidate sitting here right now. Shall I send him up to you?"

"OK".

As it happens. Do such things *just happen?* No, I believe it was God at work. Sure enough I got the job. With accommodation thrown in, on the campus. At the time I had never heard of Gresham's School, nor even knew where it was. (It is in Norfolk). It turned out to be an exciting time, because teaching of foreign languages was being revolutionised by the introduction of a new-fangled method – the language laboratory. Old hat now, but at that time the cutting edge of educational technology. It needed new teaching and learning skills, with pupils sitting with headphones, each in his or her little booth, being 'immersed' in strange sounds, soaking up a new language. All a bit hit and miss!

My school duties included supervision of boys learning to sail and play squash, so I had to be proficient in both these skills, which have given me much pleasure ever since. It was a good six years. My wife and I were able to move into a lovely home and garden of our own. A former village pub, 'The Three Horseshoes'. (I sometimes wonder how a horse can get by with only three horse-shoes).

Hill House, Stody, Norfolk. (Formerly the Three Horse Shoes pub)

COME AT ONCE

The phone rang.

 "Michael?"

"Yes."

"David here. Can you spare a moment?"

David Tuck was the curate at St Andrew's Church in Holt. We had collaborated for several years over Christian Aid Week. So I wasn't surprised to get a call.

"Michael, I want to ask you a small favour. If I send you a job-description for a chaplaincy post in Africa would you kindly write a reference for me? With your previous experience you are well placed to comment. I would appreciate your help."

The 'previous experience' was time I had spent in Tanzania in 1962/63 as the founder Headmaster of a Lutheran secondary school.

 "Fine," I said. "Glad to help".

Reading the job-description it was clear to me that David would be a good man for the job at St Mark's College, Mapanza, in Zambia, so I wrote a recommendation accordingly. What interested me most however was a brief footnote at the bottom of the page, saying "We are also looking for a Headmaster at this time."

I looked at the footnote long and hard. Was this just incidental, or was it a way that God was intervening (again) in my life? Here I was in 1969, at the age of 37, with a wife and 4 young children and a lovely home in Norfolk, in my sixth year as a teacher of Modern Languages at Gresham's School. A plum job in a top school. Why leave all this and go off to Africa again? We discussed it and came to what seemed a sensible conclusion - *send off an application and then see what happens.*

So that's what we did. With some trepidation, it must be said. Mapanza was way off the beaten track in Zambia's Southern Province. Dirt roads, with dust and potholes in the dry season and mud in the wet. 40 miles to the shops/post office/garage. St Mark's College was an old-established institution, having opened in Mapanza on the 1st of September 1932 (the day before I was born). Was God calling me to go out there?

We waited for the reply. In those days telegrams came in bright-coloured envelopes, to distinguish them from ordinary mail. The one we received from the Archbishop of Central Africa, the Rt. Rev Oliver Green-Wilkinson, was short and to the point. 3 words – "COME AT ONCE". So that settled it. I took the plunge, gave notice, bought a Land-Rover, booked a passage on a Union Castle ship to Cape Town. It meant leaving Sylvia and the children in UK for a time, until I had settled in on my own to the job at St Mark's – not easy. But the challenge was "come at once". Can't argue with that!

THE 'OCTOBER REVOLUTION'

From its foundation the purpose of St Mark's College had been teacher training. But that ended in 1953/54 when teacher training was transferred elsewhere (Chalimbana) and secondary school classes opened at Mapanza. During the 1960's new classroom blocks were constructed, also a new Dining Hall, staff houses, Science block, electricity supply with a (temperamental) generator, and improvements to the traditional 'Cubes' (square huts which served as dormitories). 1964 saw the departure of the legendary Fr. Geoffrey Fiennes after 27 years' service, just before Independence for Zambia.

For the Golden Jubilee celebrations in 2003 a Portrait of St Mark's was published, including a section on The Headmastership of Mr Michael Chesterman 1969-72:

'By 1969 things at St Mark's had reached a very low state. A reputation for strikes and violence had sadly been won, and the buildings of the main block were on the point of collapse. The Assembly Hall and stage were abandoned, the library emptied of books, an improvised office shared between the Head, deputy, typist and clerk. Acute staff shortages and massive debts painted an unhappy picture'.

Such was the situation confronting me on my arrival at Mapanza in September 1969. The teaching staff, whose morale had been under severe pressure, were encouraged by the arrival of six teachers already recruited as badly needed re-enforcements. So the combined impact of all aspects of the new regime was considerable. The account which follows is taken from my notes made after the events described, 'when the small details have receded into oblivion, leaving the highlights to stand out clearly'.

I had been recruited in hopes of turning the tide. So it was with mixed feelings of pride and apprehension that I took my first look around the school. The start of term was quickly upon us and with it my first contact with the boys. They turned out to be smart, diligent, and respectful at first sight, and things ran smoothly. I was lulled into a premature optimism. This was the examination term, when incentive to study was high. For the senior boys (Form V) it also meant a strong reluctance to undertake other duties such as a fair share of responsibilities involved in being Prefects.

As this problem worsened, my previous experience as a headmaster in Tanzania proved to be more misleading than helpful. There I had been used to a spirit of 'Harambee' – a national slogan meaning roughly 'We all pull together', where distinctions of rank counted for nothing when communal labour was called for.

The St Mark's seniors (Form Fives) however disdained physical exertion as being a distraction from their 'reading'. They preferred to exploit the availability of forced labour in Form 1, who were paraded daily for public works known as 'Trafalgar'. This curiously inappropriate name presumably derived from a superficial resemblance of the St Mark's quadrangle to Trafalgar Square in London! Insistence on self-help being contributed by seniors as well as juniors would have aroused so much antagonism that it might have been more expedient for me to let things be. However, in respect of the Vth Form a head-on collision was inevitable. They wanted to have their cake and eat it, in that they would neither continue in office themselves as Prefects nor submit to the authority of new ones. They wanted to be a law to themselves, e.g. by coming to meals as and when they pleased, deliberately and provocatively snubbing their successors.

The inevitable showdown took place outside the Dining-Hall one evening, when Form V found themselves excluded en masse for being late, with the doors closed and patrolled by staff. This led to assault and a violent rampage round the compound, necessitating the intervention of a squad of riot police from Choma and a police ultimatum to the troublemakers. They were lined up (except for some who had fled into the bush) and obliged to choose between forcible removal from the premises or signing a pledge of good conduct. They chose to sign, but even that did not save 15 of them, including the School Captain, from expulsion.

This no-nonsense approach to a serious breach of discipline was badly needed, as it exploded the dangerous tendency of Form V to believe that the imminence of their final examinations gave them virtual immunity from punishment. I was fortunate on this occasion (which was quickly nicknamed the October Revolution) to enjoy prompt and unequivocal support from the Ministry of Education. If serious offenders are automatically punished severely, even to the point of expulsion, as in this case, then everyone knows where they stand. Such swift surgical operations are preferable to expedient compromises such as re-distributing offenders to other schools. These views of mine, right or wrong, are at least not those of an armchair critic, but come straight from the hot seat behind the Headmaster's desk. (Twenty years later, when I was a Headmaster again elsewhere in Zambia, I was encouraged to find that there was a formal agreement between Head Teachers not to re-enrol expelled pupils).

The Headmaster enjoying Sports Day at St Mark's Mapanza in 1970

"SPLENDID WORK IS BEING DONE"

In the early days at St Mark's, Mapanza, when it was still a College, new boys arriving to enrol in Form 1 would first be sent to the Principal's office. Fr. Fiennes would tell the new recruit: "Go and report to the school workshop. You will there learn how to make your own desk and chair. When it is ready come and tell me, and I will inspect it. Then you can start classes".

I wanted to preserve this tradition of self-help, but I lacked the outstanding craftsmanship of Fr. Fiennes, (examples of which still remain in the school chapel). Instead, I would tell the new boy "Go to the Agricultural Science Dep't (a rather grand name for what was a tool shed), get a spade, go to the school orchard, and dig a hole. Make it deep enough so that when you stand up in it I can't see your head". In the hole the boy would plant his own guava tree, responsibility for which remained his during his time in the school. The point thus made is that we inherit assets from our predecessors and owe it to the next generation to pass on something to them.

The big event of 1971 was the Official Opening of the New Central Block on 3 April - one of those rare occasions when I have an excuse to wear my Cambridge MA gown. The construction work in 1970 had been complicated by sanctions on Rhodesia and an import ban on South African goods. The design was deliberately reminiscent in its South (front) aspect of the old brick building which it replaced – a symmetrical arcade with a large central archway aligned on the axis of the school Chapel and quadrangle. As the architect was only able to make a monthly half-day visit from his office in Lusaka 200 miles away, much of the day-to-day supervision lay in my hands. I became virtually an assistant site foreman. On the big day a guard of honour was drawn up along each side of the central path leading to and from the Chapel, where the proceedings began with a short service of thanksgiving.

The official opening of New Block at St Mark's, Mapanza, in 1971. Procession from the Chapel

The many distinguished guests then followed the VIP's to the steps of the main archway. Here the builder handed over the keys, on a velvet cushion held by the smallest Boy Scout in the school. The Hon Minister for Education, Mr Wesley Nyirenda, cut the red ribbon and unveiled a commemorative plaque.

Michael Paul Chesterman with Zambia Minister of Education, Mr Wesley Nyirenda (centre grey suit) and the Chief Education officer, Livingstone (left)

The Bishop then blessed the new buildings, and the usual round of speeches, refreshments, and traditional dancing followed. The Minister of Education was kind enough to write in the logbook as follows...."The ceremony was precise and perfect. I was impressed with the efforts the Headmaster and staff are making to make the school a good school. Splendid work is being done".

41 years later, in 2012, I revisited St Marks, and it is still going strong.

My return visit to St Mark's, Mapanza in 2012

MINISTRY OF EDUCATION

EDUCATIONAL BROADCASTING AND TELEVISION SERVICES
P.O. BOX RW.231
RIDGEWAY
LUSAKA

19th September, 1972

I am very pleased to welcome you to the Educational Broadcasting Service.

2.   You will be working as Producer for Secondary English programmes. Your duties as Producer include:-

(h)   Evaluation of programmes.   Having prepared your programmes, you will need to know how they are used in schools;   whether they are used or not at all.   We receive evaluation cards from schools but, it is one of your duties to establish how effective your work is.   You will need to visit schools to observe classes listening to educational programmes;   to discuss with teachers any difficulties they have in the use of radio progra mes, and to get ideas on how to improve the service.

Educational broadcasting – this was the new venture to which I turned my hand in September 1972, after my 3 years as Headmaster of St Mark's Secondary School. English is Zambia's national language, and English by radio was seen as a great opportunity to bring high-quality teaching of the subject into schools across the length and breadth of the country. It was creative, imaginative, and varied work. First the scripts had to be written, in line with the syllabus. Then came the challenge of recording in the studio – finding and training presenters, slotting in sound effects, getting the pauses right. The format and content of the accompanying Teachers' Notes has to be accurate, attractive, and helpful. Then comes the moment of truth, when the producer visits schools to evaluate success or failure. The optimistic assumption of those of us in the ivory tower of the headquarters of educational broadcasting was that all over Zambia thousands of pupils were listening in. *Transmitting* a programme is easy, but *reception* requires a combination of essentials – a class and teacher ready at the right time, and a portable radio in working order. Working order means *batteries*. At that time in Zambia these were in short supply. According to our surveys the serviceability ratio of school radios was as low as 50%. Despite this setback we persevered, with pre-recorded tapes available as an option. 1970's technology meant that tapes, sadly, were clumsy reel-to-reel, not cassettes. Now however (2014), distance learning in Zambia has moved forward dramatically.

One spin-off of my time as a producer was a small book I wrote – 'Say **it simply**'. Well, not a book really – it was a 30-page booklet, containing a check-list of 1500 words which I suggested should form a new 'Standard Zambian English'. It was based on Michael West's General Service List of English Words (GAL), shrunk from 2000 by excluding inappropriate words such as snow or sword. Other more appropriate words like malaria, mosquito, soap, tarmac, and kwacha found their way in.

" MICHAEL, YOU MUST GO AND SORT THINGS OUT"

This was my wife Sylvia's immediate reaction to the message we received on the phone one day in 2001. "Jerry died on 5 February".

The story goes back to my time (1969-72) as Headmaster of St Mark's College, Mapanza, in Zambia's Southern Province. We had then helped a Form 1 boy, Jerry Sibalwa, to pay his school-fees, by giving him piece-work in our garden. Subsequently we had helped him to work his way through College, get married, negotiate a mortgage to buy a house, and start a family. Jerry even named his third son after me – Michelo. In short we virtually became Ma and Pa to him.

In December 2000 we received an airmail letter from his three sons... "Things have been pretty rough. Mum passed away two years ago. Dad began losing his health, then lost his job for health reasons (kidney infection and TB), and is now bed-ridden. As a result we have been hit by a huge financial crisis. We were evicted from our home after failing to complete the mortgage payments. Ian has dropped out of his final 2nd year Diploma in Business Studies. Allen was scheduled to start an Accounts course but things took a wrong turn – no money for fees. Michelo is doing Grade 11. We don't get much help from relatives, so please, if there is any way you can help us to get out of this mess, we would appreciate it".

In response I promptly bought an air-ticket and flew out to Lusaka. The problem of AIDS orphans in Africa of course is huge. Here was a chance to help three of them. My first priority was to attend the funeral, standing alongside the 3 boys as they bore their father's coffin out of the church and to the graveside in Kabulonga. Then I had to tackle the problem faced by school dropouts – getting back into the system.

I started with Allen, by finding out first how much he owed in arrears for school-fees at Kabulonga Boys Secondary School. I then went to the bank and drew out half of that amount in kwacha. The exchange rate for Zambian kwacha at that time was such that any large sum meant a big bundle of notes. I stuffed the bundle into my hip-pocket and went off with Allen to see his Headmaster.

"Ah, Mr Chesterman, how nice to see you. How are you? And Mrs Chesterman – is she well?" In African culture you do not go straight to the point – an exchange of greetings, sometimes quite prolonged, takes precedence. After this important matter came the obvious question "And how can I help you?" I drew out from my pocket the bundle of kwacha notes and laid it on the desk. "I have a proposal for you to consider. Your pupil Allen Sibalwa is in trouble for non-payment of fees, and that is right and proper. On the table in front of you now is half the amount he owes. If you can accept that and release his certificates, then at least you recover half the outstanding fees. If however you don't agree, you get nothing back, and he loses his chance to progress. Is it a deal?"

I remember his reply. "Ah, Mr Chesterman, you are very clever! How can I refuse?" So this part of the story had a happy ending – Allen was able to enrol for college. Getting his elder brother Ian re-instated to complete his Diploma course involved a trip to Kabwe in Central Province. After several hiccups this turned out successfully. This left me with the third and last problem – getting Michelo out of the government school (Chiwala) where he was in a class of 45 and in a dormitory where facilities can best be described as 'basic'. My thoughts naturally turned to Mpelembe Secondary School in Kitwe. Why? Because I had in 1983 been its founder-Headmaster. (That's quite another story, which you can read about elsewhere in this book).

So off I went, with Michelo, for what turned out to be a providential interview with the Principal. Providential is the only word that can describe the outcome. Mr Makasa ran his finger down the class-list, with the names listed from A to Z, until he got to No 32 at the bottom – Zaloumis. He then looked up with a broad grin. "You are lucky" he said. "That boy was withdrawn last week. Michelo can have his place".

To help secure the studies of the 3 boys over future years, I opened a 'Sibalwa Trust' fund, to which many kind relatives and friends contributed generously. The investment paid off handsomely, as all three completed further education, gaining good qualifications, which in turn has resulted in good jobs. It wasn't all plain sailing, as for example degree courses at UNZA were interrupted for prolonged periods by strikes and disorders, and decent jobs were hard to find. On a recent return visit I made to Zambia imagine my delight to find my namesake and adopted grandson Michelo sitting at a posh desk on which was the label 'Assistant Personnel Officer'. Being Grandpa and Grandma to 3 AIDS orphans has been a great blessing to my wife and myself. It just shows how much difference can be made by getting involved in a small way. You can't solve all Africa's problems, but as Tesco says, "Every little helps".

The Sibalwa brothers
Michelo (Left), Allen, Ian with Nosiku and baby Jerry

TEA WITH THE SISTERS

When asked to explain what was involved in my work as General Secretary of CMAZ[1] I used to reply, jokingly, "Tea with the sisters". This referred to the warm welcome I received whenever I arrived at a mission hospital way out in the bush, after a long journey from Lusaka or elsewhere over dirt roads.

'Tea with the Sisters' in the garden at Minga Mission Hospital

---

[1] The Churches Medical Association of Zambia.

It all started one evening in 1978, towards the end of my contract as an educational broadcaster. I was chatting with a friend of mine, Dr James Cairns, Medical Officer i/c at St Francis Hospital, Katete, in East Province. Normally on his visits to Lusaka he stayed at the guest-house of the White Fathers, but as they were fully booked he asked if he could stop overnight at my home, in nearby Woodlands. James and I used to meet each other once a year at the Synod of the Diocese of Zambia to present our Annual Reports. He spoke for St Francis Hospital and I for St Mark's College. Each in turn we would report how our respective institutions were struggling for lack of funds, delays in receiving grants, staff shortages, broken-down lorries, pumps, and generators. Each in turn we would be cut short by the Bishop, congratulating us for keeping going, doing a splendid job etc.

"What in particular brings you to Lusaka this time?" I asked James. To which he replied "We have to recruit a new Chief Executive for CMAZ". James was the Chairman of CMAZ. "Oh", I said, with polite interest: "What sort of person are you looking for?"

"Someone not so old that he's past his best, but has considerable experience in administrative posts. Someone who knows Zambia from the inside, and understands how Government works here. And ideally someone with a missionary background".

This check-list immediately started to ring bells in my head. I ticked all the boxes! Age 46, with 9 years in Zambia behind me, formerly a Headmaster (twice) of Mission schools, son of a medical missionary. I applied for the job, and was appointed.

Zambia is big – a thousand miles across from end to end. Spread over its 9 Provinces at that time were 29 mission hospitals and 44 Rural Health Centres, accounting for about half of the nation's health care in rural areas. The managing agencies represented a dozen different churches, Catholic and Protestant. These were all required by the Government to 'get their act together' by forming CMAZ, so that its General Secretary could be the middleman between them and Gov't, to negotiate conditions of service, grants, drug supplies etc. Huge job!

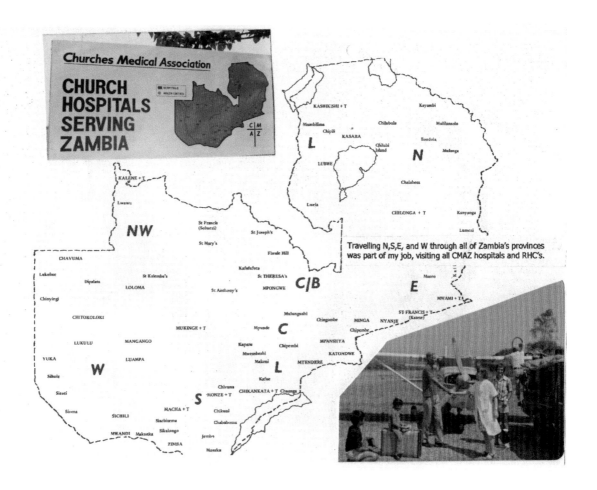

Travelling N,S,E, and W through all of Zambia's provinces was part of my job, visiting all CMAZ hospitals and RHC's.

Shortly after settling into this new 'huge job' as CMAZ Gen Sec I wrote a pamphlet. 'This appeal is addressed to all who have influence over what gets approved in Parliament. The problem is this. As long ago as 1964 His Excellency the President declared his hope that there would be the same conditions of service for all Zambian health workers irrespective of their place of work. But even now, thirteen years later (1977), this hope remains unfulfilled. Why?'

Good question. Part of the answer was lack of money. Under the system inherited from colonial times Zambian employees in church hospitals and Health Centres were paid less than their counterparts in government institutions. For example a nurse in a Government hospital, starting on scale MS15 at K.2,388 p.a., would get an annual increment of K.156, and would end up at the top of the scale on K.4,080. But the same nurse, if working in a church hospital, would just get every year the same flat-rate. Similarly, wage-rates paid to laundrymen, cooks, cleaners, and dressers in church hospitals were below those paid in Government hospitals.

In an effort to change the system, I trod the corridors of power in Lusaka. In the National Assembly I lobbied MPs when they were considering Budget estimates. Back in the CMAZ office I conferred with church leaders, who gave me good advice. "Stop asking Government for more money, Michael, because they can always say there isn't any more. Ask for justice, because they can't say there is no more justice". This tactic eventually paid off. It resulted in a Memorandum of Understanding, Article 6 of which opened as follows.....
'There shall be <u>parity of conditions of service</u> for Zambian church health workers. Approved staff in church health institutions will receive <u>equal pay and benefits as their counterparts</u> in Government institutions'.

The CHAZ (Churches Health Ass'n of Zambia) offices in Lusaka were built in 1981 in my time as Gen Sec.

I was privileged to leave behind me something in concrete, which will last !

Officially opened by the Prime Minister Hon. Nalumino Mundia

Prime site near S.End roundabout on Cairo Rd, Lusaka.

If anyone were to ask me now, in my quiet years of retirement, about what I consider to be my greatest contribution to the general good, I would rank this struggle for parity high on my list. It was my privilege to be involved in promoting a just cause. Other happy memories of my time with CMAZ abound. Imagine crossing the Kabompo river (crocodile-infested) on a dilapidated, wobbly and rickety chain-drawn 'ferry', and then stopping for a picnic lunch in the forest.

A long haul to reach the pontoon at Watopa, and a hard haul to get across. Watch out for crocs!

No improvised affair – the lady missionaries (Plymouth Brethren) brought out folding stools and table, with paper napkins and iced drinks. Grace is said, and the mosquitoes are confronted with repellent. The journey resumes, to be interrupted by a puncture, roadside repairs, and an unscheduled overnight stopover at another (Catholic) mission hospital en route. Instead of 'tea with the sisters', this time it was supper, b and b with the fathers.

When I left CMAZ in Feb 1983 I wrote a formal CMAZ Gen Sec job-description for the benefit of my successor. In it I mentioned that "there must be *forward-looking original ideas and creative thinking*". Two of my bright ideas, I am glad to say, turned out well. The

'Rotating Doctor' scheme helped to solve the problem of filling gaps when doctors in CMAZ hospitals went on leave ('furlough' in missionary jargon). They 'rotated' from one centre to the next as needed. This valuable plugging of gaps was much appreciated. Occasionally there were problems of these volunteers fitting in to the ethos of mission hospitals. I remember one colourful personality becoming rather over-friendly with a local young lady, to the extent of sharing his accommodation at Monze hospital with her. News of this came to the notice of the local Catholic Bishop, who summoned the doctor to his office. "Young man. I hear that you are living with a certain young lady. Are you married to her?" "No" came the frank reply. "Well, in that case, if you wish to continue living with her I shall marry you in church next Sunday".

Another success story was the 'Roving Mechanic' scheme, whereby a qualified mechanic complete with tools could be booked to come and fix pumps, generators, etc, and then move on to another hospital and sort out their technical problems. Essential for this purpose was a reliable 4wd Landcruiser specially fitted out. I was able to negotiate a substantial donation from Europe, and arranged delivery of the vehicle to Dar es Salaam, from where I would drive it 2,000 miles along the Great North Rd into Zambia.

I invited my son Colin to come along and join me for this adventurous trip. On the way, in Zambia's Northern Province, there is a river crossing at the Chambishi. In the rainy season the ford here becomes a raging torrent. We reached the bank and looked across. Did I dare risk our precious new vehicle being swept away downstream? How would I account to the donors for its loss, if the worst happened? Colin settled it straightaway. "Come on, Dad, where's the stuff that made the Empire?" Of course I had to rise to the occasion, and we made it safely across!

Another big challenge was the need for CMAZ to own its own purpose-built premises, rather than muddle along in rented offices a long way out from Lusaka city-centre. That project too came to fruition, thanks to a generous grant negotiated with Bread from the World in Germany. I found myself heavily involved with architects and builders as the new CMAZ building took shape. In addition to work in the office there was also a <u>CMAZ guest-house</u> to be run, by my wife, at our home in the Lusaka suburb of Roma. Staff from CMAZ member-hospitals and Health Centres needed somewhere to stay during essential visits to Lusaka from their remote outposts. With all this, and more, going on every day, there was never a dull moment!

High-speed trip across Lake Bangweulu to reach Lubwe Mission. In the middle you are out of sight of land. Don't have engine failure !

"WHY DON'T YOU APPLY?"

During my ten years in Lusaka I used to keep fit by playing squash once a week. One evening, as I was leaving the Sports Club, I glanced up at the notice-board. Something new caught my eye. "Entries invited for the 1982 Veteran's Championship, to be held at the Nkana Club in Kitwe. Entrance qualification – Age 50 or over". As I was born in 1932 I just qualified. So I sent in my entry, and in due course made the 4-hour drive up to the Copperbelt.

In the semi-final I lost to an Nkana Club member, Trevor Watson, in a hard match. You know how it is – after the match and a shower your opponent invites you to have a drink in the bar, and you chat.

"What's your job, Trevor?"

"I'm the Assistant Manager of CET – The Copperbelt Education Trust".

"Oh. What does that involve?"

"At present we are planning to open a big new secondary school, and are advertising for a suitably qualified Headmaster".

"Oh, really? I was formerly a Headmaster".

"Well then. Why don't you apply?"

On the long drive back to Lusaka next day these words kept ringing through my head. "Why don't you apply?" I was nearing the end of my time as Gen Sec of CMAZ. Was this the opportunity to remain in Zambia while taking on a new challenge? I pulled in to a lay-by in the shade, and mouthed a short prayer "Is this you speaking, Lord?" Back came the reply "You just send the application in, and leave the rest to me".

Somewhat to my surprise, I was soon called for interview at CET in Kitwe. When invited by the panel to ask them any questions, I said "Copper-mining is big business. Huge machines, belching furnaces, refineries. I know nothing of all that. My values come from my experience in mission work".

"That is precisely why we short-listed you for the job, Mr Chesterman. Leave the bulldozers and dump-trucks for us to handle. You just run the school according to your standards. Turn out the skilled young men and women we need to send on to university for degrees. You will be starting from scratch – setting up the curriculum, advising on the new buildings, site development, boarding arrangements, teaching and domestic staff, budget – the whole package".

How could I refuse? A blank sheet on which I was invited to make my mark. So it was that I became a small cog in the giant set-up of ZCCM – Zambia Consolidated Copper Mines. The new school was to be called **Mpelembe**

Mpelembe School, Kitwe, Zambia

IN AT THE DEEP END.

So it was that on 5 January 1983 I received a letter from the Manager Education, "I offer my congratulations at being selected to undertake what will be a challenging but also a most satisfying job. The school will open on Tuesday March 1st 1983."

Part of the challenge was that the school wasn't even built yet. No classrooms ready on the new site, no dormitories. My Headmaster's office was my briefcase, with all my paperwork inside it. Everything had to be improvised. The pupils were accommodated in vacant hostels at Wusikili Mine Hospital, several miles away, and were shuttled to and fro in busloads. We borrowed classrooms from the ZCCM Primary School which was adjacent to the new Mpelembe Secondary School site, so we were able to watch the graders and the bulldozers and the heavy trucks trundle by. One of my vivid memories is recalled in a photo of a big hole in the ground, destined to be the school swimming-pool. A tractor hauling a heavy load of excavated soil and rock is left hanging precariously over the hole, so the caption reads 'In at the deep end'.

'In at the deep end' was not just a figure of speech. During the construction there were many pitfalls.

The same could perhaps be said of my role as the founder-Headmaster. I ended up being responsible for 670 pupils, all the teaching staff, and for 100 ancillary staff on the boarding and maintenance side – matrons, cooks, cleaners, gardeners, watchmen...

Mpelembe Secondary School at full strength – 670 of us.

A particularly memorable day was the school's Official Opening on Thursday 8th September 1983 by His Excellency the President of Zambia, Dr Kenneth Kaunda. Such was the scale of the top brass in ZCCM (Zambia Consolidated Copper Mines) at that time that I found myself ranked below 100 in the order of precedence!

Protocol was strict. There was an opening Hymn, the first line of which was 'Let there be peace on earth'. (At the time of writing this book, 31 years later in August2014, this has a contemporary relevance, with so much death and destruction going on in the Gaza strip, Syria, and elsewhere). Then of course there had to be traditional dancing, presentation of mementoes by no less than 10 General Managers, and a bouquet of flowers from the Head Girl. Next came singing of the patriotic song 'Tiyende pamodzi', robustly led by the President, waving as always his white handkerchief. His Excellency then made his Address, reminding the audience that at the time of Independence (in 1964) there was only one Zambian who held a degree in Engineering. Now (1983) over 600 Zambian graduates worked in the mines.

After the President unveiled a commemorative plaque came my brief moment in the limelight. It was my duty and privilege as Headmaster to step forward and hand to KK a golden ballpoint pen, for him to write an appropriate entry in the school's Logbook. Fame at last!

President Kaunda (K.K.) officially opening Mpelembe Secondary School. Kitwe, in 1983.

Talking of fame, I was somewhat eclipsed at Mpelembe by the exploits of my wife. Sylvia had previously, during our time in Lusaka, been the national coach for the Zambian Women's Athletics team. Now was her opportunity to make the most of the new sports field under construction on the flatter ground between the main campus and the Kafue river. The facilities included a 400m track, so athletics was very much on the agenda. In addition to PE lessons on the timetable for Mpelembe students, Sylvia organised an athletics club open to boys and girls from the nearby townships such as Ndeke. The programme for track events included hurdling, which of course meant a need for hurdles. This problem was solved by improvisation – using bamboo cut from the clumps growing on the banks of the river nearby. Just cut two short lengths of bamboo, tie them together to form an inverted V, then add a crosspiece. Sylvia soon noticed that one 15-year old boy in particular, Samuel Matete, was showing a remarkable natural talent. With the benefit of Sylvia's coaching in those early stages he went on improving his performance, so much so that 8 years later, in 1991 at Tokyo, he became World Champion for 400m Men's Hurdles. 3 years later in Canada he became Commonwealth Games champion, and then he crowned it all with a Silver Medal in the 1996 Olympics at Atlanta, with a time of 47.78 seconds.

Another lasting achievement of Sylvia's at Mpelembe was the landscape gardening and tree-planting, into which she poured much skill. Just walk around the campus today and enjoy the beauty of the jacarandas along the avenues and the terraces. The sloping site allows views down over the sports field and fishponds to the river-bank. In the evening you hear the hippos in the Kafue grunting as they emerge to browse. Another spectacular view on the distant horizon at night-time was of the red-hot slag from the Nkana mine being tipped out of the hoppers on the little railway.

A by-product from our time at Mpelembe was that we extended our family by becoming 'Ma and Pa' to the School Captain Joshua Ngoma and Head Girl Susan, after they got married. I used to delegate a lot of responsibility to Joshua, and together we presided in rather a grand manner over School Assemblies. When Joshua was in the UK, studying geology at the Royal School of Mines in Camborne, Sylvia and I attended his graduation 'in loco parentis', and we have kept in touch over the years. He was not surprisingly snapped up by the mines in South Africa for a top job in the rainbow nation. While we were on a visit to Johannesburg he surprised us when we stopped in traffic behind a big builders' lorry. "I bought that company last week, after it went bust". Shrewd move in the year before South Africa hosted the World Cup. It paid off handsomely as the construction industry boomed. Good for him!

Leading the way, with my School Captain Joshua alongside. These 6th Formers went on to take engineering degrees at British Universities. Very rewarding.

HOT SEAT.

It is in the nature of things that Headmasters are at times called upon to handle difficult situations and make tough decisions. Take for example the problem sitting on my desk at Mpelembe in November 1983. I found myself having to write a letter to the Acting Chairman of ZCCM (Zambia Consolidated Copper Mines), starting as follows "I am sorry to have to inform you that your son Anthony is in serious trouble". The 'trouble' was that Anthony, a Grade 11 pupil, had been caught red-handed after stealing examination papers from pigeonholes in the staffroom and then cheating in the exams. For such a serious offence the penalty had to be either expulsion or voluntary withdrawal of the pupil from school by the parent. A somewhat awkward interview in my office ensued, (awkward because I was an employee of ZCCM myself, now facing their top man, way above me in the ladder). Fortunately Anthony's father chose the latter option. Despite this, the Times of Zambia of 3 Dec 1983 front-page story was entitled 'Mpelembe expels exam cheat', The article went on to say that the school 'was under pressure from angry parents', and that 'the boy had to be expelled to retain the good name of the institution'. At the time I was commended by staff for having done the right thing and there were no immediate repercussions.

Fast forward through 1984, to the end of January 1985. I opened the post, and there was a letter from my eldest son Graham, a teacher in the UK. In it was an enclosure – a clip from the Overseas Vacancies pages of the Times Educational Supplement of 18th January. The advertisement was for 'Headmaster Secondary School Central Africa'. Graham's cryptic comment was "Dad, - interesting?" From the job-description it was clear that it could only be Mpelembe. It was my job up for grabs, without my knowing!

OVERSEAS CONT

Head Master
Secondary School
Central Africa

Our client is looking for a Headmaster with experience of running a secondary boarding school, with good scholarship, firm ideas on school discipline, business sense and general administrative ability, have a wide range of interests and be able and willing to share in curricular and extra-curricular activities. The school has been established to provide high quality education, with the emphasis on Mathematics and Science up to University entrance level. A well qualified team of Heads of Departments and specialised teachers provide the necessary staff to ensure the achievement of objectives.

Preference will be given to applications from holders of a B.Sc or B.A. degree plus P.G.C.E., with experience overseas.

The salary is negotiable, with about 60% paid free of tax in the U.K. and contracts of two or three years are mutually renewable. Excellent accommodation, return air fares for the successful candidate and his family, provision for education, free life assurance and a superb climate complement the overall package.

Confidential Reply Service: Please write with full CV quoting reference 1919/JE on your envelope, listing separately any company to whom you do not wish your details to be sent. CV's will be forwarded directly to our client, who will conduct the interviews. Charles Barker Recruitment Limited, 30 Farringdon Street, London EC4A 4EA.

CHARLES BARKER
ADVERTISING · SELECTION · SEARCH

TIMES GO SUPPLEMENT 18/1/85.
Dad - INTERESTING? - graham

Next day, Friday 3rd February, I went to the CET (Copperbelt Educational Trust) office and asked the Manager what was going on. He 'categorically denied' any knowledge of the advertising of my job. Obviously therefore the responsibility for it lay higher up in the chain of command. Sure enough 2 days later I was handed a letter signed by the General Manager of ZCCM. "You are hereby given 3 months' notice of termination of service, and you will therefore work your last shift on 4 May 1985".

Work your last shift. Nice phrase. No explanation or reason given, but there was at least some sugar on the pill "We would like to express our thanks for your services and wish you success in your future endeavours". A follow-up letter a fortnight later from the Personnel Manager 'clarified the position' by stating that "it is not an obligation on either party to disclose the reason(s) for terminating the contract".

Move on a fortnight to the AGM of the Mpelembe Parent Teachers Association, attended by 32 members of staff and 150 parents on 2nd March. The Minutes record that under 'Matters arising from the Headmaster's Report' a spokesman for the parents commented that "The termination of the Headmaster's contract has shocked us". Under CET Manager's Remarks there was reference to 'the Headmaster's powerful statement and the consternation among the parents'. This perhaps explains the bombshell in a letter delivered to me by the Manager 3 days later on 5th March. "It has been decided that your employment should be terminated with immediate effect, therefore your last working day will be Tuesday 5 March". In other words, you have the rest of the afternoon to clear your desk, hand over, and move out.

So we had no choice but to pack up and go. There were however some interesting developments before we finally flew back from Zambia to UK. During a brief stop-over in Lusaka Sylvia and I decided to make a courtesy call on the Minister for Education, to say goodbye. Both of us had previously had dealings with Kebby Musokotwane, when he had been Minister for Sport and Minister of Finance. He had also officially visited Mpelembe School and written favourable comments about it. So on 16th April we called in at his office and in response to his enquiries briefed him on how our contract had been abruptly terminated. To our astonishment he promptly picked up the red telephone on his desk, his hot line to the President at State House. When the conversation was over, to our even greater astonishment he said "His Excellency the President has directed that you hang on for a while, so that he can look into the matter". So our final departure from Zambia had to be delayed. In the event nothing further came of this top-level intervention. But the opening sentence of the letter the Minister chose to write that day to the President, Dr Kaunda, warmed our hearts. "I was close to tears when Mr Michael Chesterman narrated his ordeal with ZCCM when he was saying goodbye to me this morning".

As things turned out, this was not to be our 'final' departure from Zambia. Twelve years later I was to find myself dramatically becoming a Headmaster in Kitwe again! (But that's another story, - for you to catch up with later in this book if you like). Looking back in hindsight, I see remarkable parallels between my story and the fall and then rise back to high office of Joseph in the Bible. He was framed by Potiphar's wife for an offence he didn't commit, imprisoned, then promoted to be governor over Egypt, with a gold chain round his neck (Genesis 41, v.42). In the imposing foyer of the new Assembly Hall at Mpelembe pupils and visitors can see a Roll of Honour of Headmasters - and there, heading the list, is my name, written in letters of gold!

WHAT NOW?

After 16 years in Zambia, here I was in April 1985, with my wife Sylvia, back in UK. Fortunately we owned a lovely home and garden in North Norfolk, in which we were able to 'resettle', as they say. Our three sons were all in good jobs, and our daughter was in her final year at University. Fine. Problem - how was I going to earn a living?

The answer was surprising. People who lived near us in the Briston and Holt area soon found a leaflet in their letter-boxes. Smart gold logo with initials GB at the top of a discreet light grey page. The opening line of the text was "I may be able to help you over a problem which faces many retired people. The problem is this – Are my savings invested in the best possible way?" Lower down the page came the punchline. "Gunson Bell Associates with whom I am a consultant is a local firm who specialise in giving advice on financial matters. If you are interested and would like to have a chat either ring the Office or contact me at my home. Yours sincerely, M. P. Chesterman".

A consultant. A financial adviser. Me? Well, actually, Yes. Strange things can happen! A friend of mine at Sheringham Baptist Church had greeted me after the morning service. "Welcome back from Africa, Michael. What are you going to do now?" To which the truthful reply was "I don't know". His immediate response took me unawares, to say the least. "My business is expanding. If you would like to join my small team of financial advisers I could give you on-the-job training. You have an honest face, and I think elderly people would trust you not to take them for a ride".

So, I took him at his word and plunged in. (At that time anyone could set up as a financial adviser without a formal licence or qualification). I printed a business card, and a hand-out telling people "You'll find us easily in Briston – just across the road from the Post Office". As my client list steadily grew, so did my job-satisfaction. Sure enough, there were lots of people out there who found decisions over money matters confusing and difficult. Jargon such as bid-offer spreads, yield, etc needed clear explanation, which clients appreciated. I ended up with 40 clients, holding between them portfolios worth over £400,000, which needed periodic monitoring. In September 1986, by which time I had moved to a new job in London, my last Newsletter told them "There have been no losers since I started giving investment advice. Your original £400,000 is now worth over half a million". You could say I was just fortunate to have operated at a time when share prices and fund values were rising steadily. True, but nonetheless I am glad to have helped by giving good advice. How many financial advisers these days can boast that there have been "no losers"?

pioneer
Magazine of the AFRICA EVANGELICAL FELLOWSHIP

OUT OF AFRICA

There is always something new out of Africa, so they say. Well, the latest export from the dark continent has just arrived in the Wimbledon office after over a year in transit – the new General Secretary of AEF, Great Britain.

Yes, it was in June last year that my wife, Sylvia, and I left Zambia after 16 happy years there in a variety of jobs. These included being headmaster of a mission secondary school, an educational broadcaster and an administrator responsible for coordinating the work of 80 mission hospitals and health centres. With such a background (quite apart from a missionary tradition in the family already) it is hardly surprising that the opportunity to join AEF presented a call which came to me as straight from the Lord. As Abraham's servant put it, *'I being in the way, the Lord led me.'*

It is a long way (not in distance but in lifestyle and surroundings) from our Norfolk home and my recent year's work as a financial advisor to the very different demands of an AEF executive post. There is the big challenge of the AEF motto, 'God First – Go Forward'. Forward, but the question is – where to? AEF is poised on the eve (only a couple of years away) of its centenary. New horizons stretch ahead towards which we in the office and you 'out there' must move together under the leadership of

the Council and the direction of God.

As I take over the so-called 'burden of office' I acknowledge my indebtedness to the large number of wellwishers who have expressed their support. Without such backing no chief executive can survive, let alone succeed. I also owe thanks to my colleagues – the back-up team who quietly and conscientiously do most of the uninspiring paperwork without getting front-page treatment in the magazine. Think of that well-known phrase, 'Two heads are better than one.' Well, that is what we have now, with me at one desk and Dorothy Haile (ex-headmistress) at another! Let us hope the saying works out true. I am sure it will.

In the harsh glare of publicity surrounding current events, Africa is in the news. Right there in the thick of it all is the universal church. The darker the situation the brighter is the light of the Gospel. Right there too is AEF in the front line with the Bible. Missionary endeavour is not an out of date anachronism, no quaint relic of a bygone era. It is a calling to stir your heart. Despite the lack of glamour, office work and administration is part of the whole enterprise ●

Michael & Sylvia Chesterman

You readers too – we are all in this together. Keep praying and giving. The printed page links us, despite the miles in between. So I greet you as fellow-workers and look forward to meeting many of you in person as time goes by.

MICHAEL CHESTERMAN   General Secretary

October – December 1986 Number 4 Volume 100

God First — Go Forward

Serving Christ in
ANGOLA	BOTSWANA
GABON	MALAWI
MAURITIUS	MOZAMBIQUE
NAMIBIA	REUNION
SOUTH AFRICA	SWAZILAND
ZAMBIA	ZIMBABWE

Potential Fields:
MADAGASCAR

BRITISH ISLES & EUROPE Headquarters
Africa Evangelical Fellowship
30 Lingfield Road
LONDON SW19 4PU
Telephone
01-946 1176/947 3636

General Secretary
M P Chesterman

Admin & Personnel Secretary
Miss D M Haile

Finance Officer
J D Evans

AEF Representatives
Scotland   Mrs E Russell
144 Stewarton Street.
WISHAW ML2 8AG

N Ireland & Eire   A B Gordon
24 Woodcroft Park
HOLYWOOD BT18 0PS
Telephone: Holywood (023 17) 3284
Europe   W Brandle
2 rue du Marechal Fayolle
94130 Nogent-sur-Marne, FRANCE
Telephone: (1) 4876 20 08
Zimbabwe Committee
Chairman   A Mitchell
Box 8164. Causeway, Harare

British Council
Chairman: Dr R Schram
J A Baldock	Rev J Budgen
Miss J Clayton	Mrs D J Crowther
G W Davies	Rev E Forward
W O Graham	Rev G Grogan
J S I Hayworth	G P Holloway
Lady Richardson	R A Lucas
Dr B Stanley	F R I Sowerby
	S Steenson

International Headquarters
Reading, England
International Director: Dr R Foster

Other Sending Councils
in the USA, Canada, South Africa,
Australia, New Zealand

The front page of the Oct-Dec 1986 issue of 'Pioneer', the quarterly magazine of AEF -the Africa Evangelical Fellowship

The front page article describes as 'hardly surprising' my decision to accept in August 1986 appointment as its General Secretary. It also points out that office work and administration in a 'sending' country is part of the whole missionary enterprise. My reference in the article to 'lack of glamour' derives perhaps partly from the fact that the accommodation provided for us was a house in Wandsworth, opposite a huge cemetery and not far from the famous prison!

For the next five years I led the small team in the AEF office in leafy Wimbledon. Dorothy handled personnel matters, John the finance, Juliet the publicity. I was the man on the road (the travelling salesman you might say), out and about visiting supporting churches, families of our 40 missionaries, Bible colleges, conferences. Preaching engagements such as just down the road in Battersea or across the water in Belfast. Speaking engagements as far apart as Berwick and Birmingham.

Only about half of my time was spent at my desk in the AEF office.

BRITISH SAFARI..

During 1989 the General Secretary, Michael Chesterman, plans to be on tour around the regions as follows:

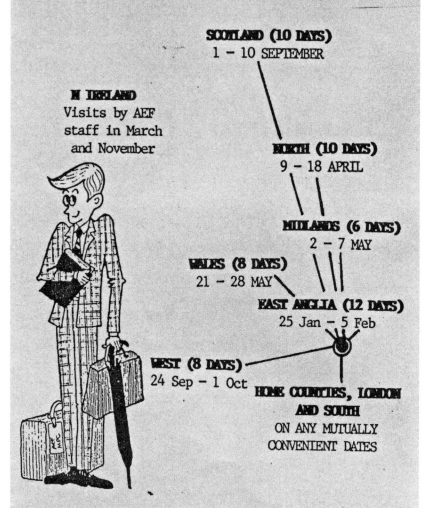

SCOTLAND (10 DAYS)
1 - 10 SEPTEMBER

N IRELAND
Visits by AEF
staff in March
and November

NORTH (10 DAYS)
9 - 18 APRIL

MIDLANDS (6 DAYS)
2 - 7 MAY

WALES (8 DAYS)
21 - 28 MAY

EAST ANGLIA (12 DAYS)
25 Jan - 5 Feb

WEST (8 DAYS)
24 Sep - 1 Oct

**HOME COUNTIES, LONDON
AND SOUTH**
ON ANY MUTUALLY
CONVENIENT DATES

At these places and times, Michael will be 'on call' to help you if you ask. There are lots of possibilities: a missionary greeting or message during a Sunday service or mid-week meeting, a prayer group, morning/afternoon, evening, at home/church/college/wherever. Maybe a missionary weekend or simply a showing of our new video, produced jointly by AIM and AEF, featuring Namibia and entitled "The Heart of the Matter". It lasts 15 minutes and is an eye-opener. All you have to do is ask for it and we'll post it to you on free loan.

Also occasional trips to the 'field' - places scattered around many countries in Africa.

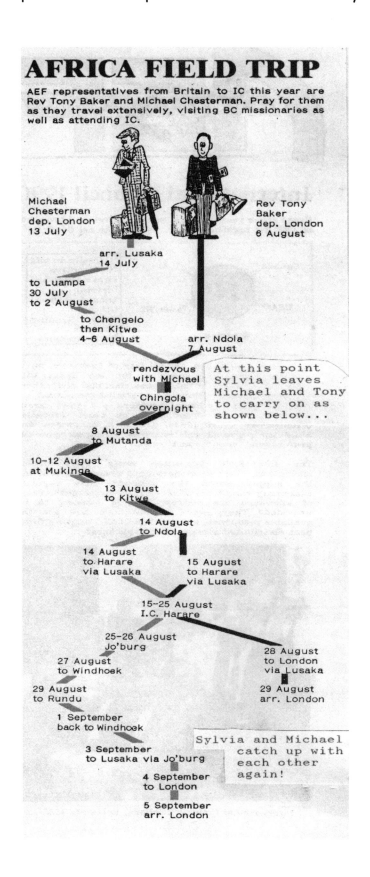

AEF'S programme for SSTMs[2] enabled young people to join in. Stephen Bishop here at Luampa Hospital supervises unloading of milk powder.

AEF was international with 6 Sending Councils whose leaders met in Harare, with International Director Dr. Foster.

---

[2] Special Short Term Missionaries

My travel schedule for July/August/September 1987 started with Paris and a flight to Libreville in Gabon to meet and greet Gabonese church leaders. Then up-country (rough going) to a remote AEF mission-station recently opened up by Dr David and Jane Mann at Oyem. Dense forest, palm-trees, mosquitoes.

I then took a week off AEF duty for a private trip to what was then called Zaire, to visit the BMS mission station at Yakusu, where my parents had worked, and where I had spent early childhood between 1932 and 1936. To my astonishment some dear old African women at the 'welcome back' party in Yakusu rushed forwards and gave me a big hug. They had been my nannies 55 years previously, when I had been just a toddler! Then they stood back, looked at me carefully and said "Comme il rassemble a son père!" (How like his father he is!). Was this recognition of me as a chip off the old block? In the village, on the banks of the mighty river (formerly Congo then renamed Zaire), one very old man, half-blind, pulled out a battered old notebook. In it he had recorded notes of sermons preached by my father back in the 1930's. What a tribute to the work of missionaries, and proof that the rewards of their labour last long!

Back on my AEF duties my notes record that the trail led to Johannesburg, a 5-hour drive to the 'rocky highlands' of Swaziland, the AEF International Council in Bulawayo, the plains of Malawi, and lastly back to Zambia. My comment at the time "What a wealth of experiences" just about sums up my time with AEF. This came to an end in August 1991, when we returned 'home' to our secluded corner of North Norfolk.

BACK IN AFRICA AGAIN.

The man in front of the computer desk in the B.E.S.O. office in London tapped away for a while and then struck the 'Enter' key. Now guess what? My name appeared on his screen. Surprise? No, not really. B.E.S.O. stands for British Executive Services Overseas. They maintain a register of experts in many fields, available to go out virtually anywhere in the world, to advise agencies in developing countries how to manage development projects. Dam-building, hospitals, railways, universities, airports – you name it, and B.E.S.O will have a consultant on hand. I was on their list, in the category of education in Africa. Chengelo secondary school in Zambia had applied to B.E.S.O. for a specialist to take over as Acting Headmaster. Was I available?

The answer was Yes, I was. The vacancy was short-term, to stand in for 4 months while the founder Headmaster of Chengelo, Neil Solomon, took well-earned leave. There was however more to it than just keeping the show on the road. The Board of Governors saw the need for someone with appropriate experience to advise them and make an in-depth appraisal of progress and policy going forward as the school developed. It was an exciting story – in just over 3 years from its opening in 1988 to enrolment of 200+. A farmer's field becoming a new purpose-built school campus.

March 1992....I'm writing this after dark, by the light of an emergency car-battery strip light, rigged up just outside the mosquito net in our bedroom. The generator packed up this morning; when I went to have a look I was amazed it has kept going so long. Ah well, supper by candlelight can be seen as romantic, the fridge works on paraffin, and the solar-powered torch we brought with us was a good buy.

My wife Sylvia has found plenty of scope and is not just 'tagging along'. Out there in the field beyond the water-furrow she is methodically pegging out an athletics track, strategically sited between the anthills. (After smoking out the snakes from them). Also careful plans are made to fit in football and rugby pitches, basketball, netball, and volleyball courts. Hot work under the sun! Two tractors with mud-scoops, grass-cutting blades, and hay-rakes add power and pace to the process. The inside lane on the 400m track turned out to be accurate to within just a few cm. Marvellous!

April 1992...It's all happening. We had just got onto our stride, when sickness struck. As more and more of the students went down with weakness and vomiting, followed by some of the staff, we realised that this was not just a few cases of malaria, but something more serious. First I sent 28 of the boarders home, while we carried on as best we could with depleted staff. The tell-tale signs of yellow faces, and a visit from the school doctor, confirmed that we were up against an outbreak of Hepatitis A. So I had to close the school. This meant sending 200 boys and girls home without notice (telephones don't work reliably out here in the bush). Buses etc have to be arranged. Staff families have to be protected with gamma-globulin injections. I am now filling more gaps than one. The Deputy Head, Bursar, and Accounts Manager are all resting, out of action. Is this confirmation that I was 'called' to be here?

I ceremonially planted this flame tree in the Hostel forecourt in 1992, and look at it now, 9 years later !

The Chilangoma hills provide a dramatic backdrop to the campus at Chengelo.

Cross-country at Chengelo means a run up to the cross on the hill and back before breakfast on Saturdays.

May 1992...When things got back to normal I tried an interesting experiment. The lawn in front of the Dining-hall was spoilt by patches of rough 'couch' grass. One day I said to the Prefects "If I go down on my hands and knees on the grass outside the Dining-Hall at break-time, will you step forward and join me weeding by hand? If everyone sees the Headmaster and Prefects giving a lead, how can they refuse to join in?" Risky – but it worked! On another occasion, when returning hoes and spades to the foreman in charge of the tool shed, I commented about turning the area into 'Chengelo Park'. "No" he replied, "It will be like the Garden of Eden!" Back in the office I plugged away with plans, projects, paperwork, timetables, curriculum, budget, even searching (unsuccessfully) for Peugeot wheel-rims. All part of the job.

July 1992... I 'signed off', and handed the school back to a grateful Neil Solomon.

Oh Yes, there is one other episode from my time in 1992 as Headmaster at Chengelo that I think is worth recalling. I was in the office one morning when the phone rang. I picked up the receiver and a voice said "Chiluba here". I was a bit taken aback, and hesitated before replying. Frederick Chiluba was after all the President of Zambia. Was it *him* on the line? Well, Yes – it really was him. "Mr Chesterman, can you kindly do me a favour?" I was even more taken aback. Do the President a favour. How? "Mr Chesterman, I have a problem. My son Castro has just been expelled from his school for misconduct. I would very much appreciate it if you could give him a place at Chengelo. Could you come down to State House so that we can talk about it?"

So, down I went to Lusaka. We sat there, the President of Zambia and I, in his office. It was a friendly man-to-man discussion. Like two fathers having a chat (which of course it was). "Castro is waiting outside – will you speak to him?" In he came, very subdued and respectful. I came straight to the point. "Young man, you should be ashamed of yourself. Here is your father, carrying the burden of high office. And what do you do? Instead of helping him, you add to his problems. Now he is asking me to give you a second chance. You don't deserve it, but if you promise me here and now to turn over a new leaf, we will give it a try. But if you step out of line at school, that's it – you'll be out. Is that clearly understood? "Yes, Sir". A grateful President then invited me to stay for tea, and a photograph on the steps of State House. I am tall and he is short, and I remember how I had to stand two steps below him so that our heads were level.

With President Chiluba on the steps of State House in Lusaka, Zambia

Sadly this story does not have a happy ending. Not long after I left Chengelo, Castro had to be expelled. Sadly also President Chiluba himself later fell from grace, with allegations of corruption swirling around. A double tragedy.

On a more cheerful note, in my closing report to the Governors I was upbeat. I said "It is a tremendous achievement for non-professionals (i.e. commercial farmers) to have constructed a boarding school in the bush, on a shoestring budget. All this on top of having their own farms to manage". The success story is still going strong.

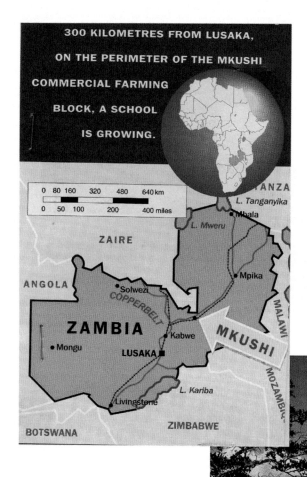

300 KILOMETRES FROM LUSAKA, ON THE PERIMETER OF THE MKUSHI COMMERCIAL FARMING BLOCK, A SCHOOL IS GROWING.

A mixture of miombo woodland and developed farmland surrounds the school. Overlooked by the Chilongoma hills, no school could ask for a more idyllic setting. Gardens and lawns complement the attractive layout of the four hostels which house 250 pupils. The dining hall and staff houses complete the picture of a school that has become an established landmark in central Zambia. The carefully designed classroom and administration complex looks towards the playing fields, squash, tennis, and basketball courts and the 25m x 12m swimming pool.

Back in England, I became Treasurer of CET, the Chengelo Educational Trust. In that capacity in 1994 I submitted a project application to Bread for the World (Brot fur die Welt), a large German mission agency, for a substantial grant with which to establish a School Farm. It made sense for Chengelo to have its own farm, which could both feed the school and be a model training farm for agricultural science. The following account of what happened is taken from p.140 of the official history of Chengelo School – a paperback by Jeremy Collingwood, published in 2006:

"The application was sent in August to the head office in Stuttgart. No reply was received. A polite reminder was submitted. But by Christmas there was still no reply. So Michael decided to take the bull by the horns. He booked a flight to Stuttgart and asked for an appointment on 6th January for himself and Traugott Hartmann, a school Governor, who was then on leave in Germany. The day dawned. It was bitterly cold. Michael and Traugott turned up at the Bread for the World offices, to find them closed. 'Heute geschlossen' - closed today. It was Epiphany, a public holiday. There was nothing for it but to swallow the disappointment and fly home empty-handed. The delay continued without any apparent progress. Then, on 27th March 1995 Michael got a surprise telephone call. "Mr Chesterman?" "Yes". "This is Mr Hess – the man you never met! I am pleased to inform you that our allocation Board has approved an amount of DM 50.000 for the Chengelo Training Farm". Michael's reaction; WOW! Fifty thousand marks – that's over £20,000!"

From small beginnings the farm grew to become a major production unit – vegetables, poultry, pigs, dairy, beef, cattle, orchard, and demonstration plots. Now move on another 5 years, to 2000. The need now was for a tractor – essential for producing maize in bulk. This time I adopted a different approach – fund-raising in my home area of Norfolk. Visitors to local agricultural shows were handed a leaflet, telling them: "A farm like this needs a tractor like this (Massey-Ferguson 240)". Progress toward the target of £10,000 was made, but then the project seemed to stall. It's the last lap that is always the hardest.

A FARM LIKE THIS

NEEDS A TRACTOR LIKE THIS

This is where I drew a blank in Stuttgart, at the offices of Bread for the World, in 1985. 6th January (Epiphany) is a public holiday in Germany. The office was closed, so I never met their Mr Hess. Happy ending however – the grant application (for the Chengelo School Farm) was approved (£20,000).

I went down to near London (Chorleywood) for the christening of my granddaughter. Lots of expensive posh cars in the church car-park. At the base of one of the pillars in the church a plain wooden box. "What's that for?" "Oh, it's our Lazarus box, for special projects in aid of good causes". "What project are you currently sponsoring?" "Oh, we've just finished one, and are looking for another". Of course you can guess what happened – by Christmas the tractor was paid for and on its way.

David Moffat donated the land for the school (part of his farm) and was a driving force behind the construction programme.

Neil Solomon (front-right in the white suit) and Sylvia with staff and students.

It was my privilege to 'stand in' for Neil Solomon for 4 months as Acting Head and keep the school ticking over.

Sylvia also had a key role in the PE department

"PERFECT FOR OUR REQUIREMENTS"

Skip over the years 1993-95 as being for me relatively unexciting (compared to the turbulent times before and afterwards). I taught at Bushey Place School in Aylsham, and then in the Modern Languages Dep't at King Edward's School, King's Lynn. Then in February 1996, out of the blue you might say, I was contacted by B.E.S.O. (British Executive Services Overseas). They had received a request from Lechwe School, a private school in Kitwe, Zambia, for an adviser to help with preparations for Sixth Form and their first intake of boarding students in Sept 1996. They put forward my name. The reply on 15 Feb from the Headmistress, Mrs Lin Williams was "Mr Chesterman's qualifications and experience are *perfect for our requirements.*" The prospect of a return to Kitwe appealed to us (Remember we had been there at Mpelembe School in 1983/85). We accepted the assignment, and flew out in March.

On arrival we found that there had already been an intake of 28 boy boarders, on an improvised basis, in a rented house near the school. My wife and I were put in charge as Houseparents of this 'Hostel', with its grandiose name of 'Marquesia Lodge'. It was so overcrowded that some of the boys 'spilled over' on to mattresses on the floor, or into a caravan by the back door. Water supply was at best intermittent, and at times restricted to what could be imported by bucket. All very makeshift, but we managed.

Living conditions at this time in the Boys Hostel were difficult. The opening of new kitchens on the main school campus meant that we had to climb on board the school bus at 06.45 hrs in time for breakfast, and then have a long (12-hr) day, with lunch, afternoon classes, Prep, supper on the patio by the swimming-pool, and showers (because of the water-shortage in the Hostel). My diary for November records that "the gang of labourers outside has just succeeded, (miraculously, to judge from the shouting and confusion) in lifting the new water-storage-tank onto its supports. If, by another miracle, the new borehole delivers water into it, with all pumps and valves working, that will enhance the quality of life here immeasurably". Talking about the quality of life in Zambia at that time, my diary records that in the shops in Kitwe there were posters which read: "Owing to the current economic climate, the light at the end of the tunnel has been switched off". Ah well, you may as well laugh as cry!

So we moved into 1997. My diary for January noted "At school the Bursar has been fired – a long overdue remedy for financial mismanagement and who knows what else? They are keeping very tight-lipped about it all". The new on-campus Girls Hostel opened (on the Headmistress's insistence) before it was ready – "sewage pipes not connected, roof one-quarter open to the sky. Last-minute lick of paint, potted plants everywhere, and gushing smiles from the Headmistress as sceptical parents ploughed through the mud (no vehicles could get near)". Perhaps it is not surprising that the Board of Governors saw fit to release in February a statement to parents that "school affairs are now running smoothly and most difficulties have been resolved. The Board has absolute confidence in the management of the school under the dynamic leadership of the Headmistress". Just read between the lines of this "All is well" message and you can't help wondering what is going on behind the scenes.

My diary entry for 16 April turned out to be prophetic: "The new Term may be full of surprising, even dramatic, events. Long overdue investigations are bringing to light financial irregularities which must surely call for decisive action. Rumours abound". The abrupt departure of one of the two Deputy Heads, with hasty goodbyes, was officially described by the Board of Governors in the Parents' Newsletter as being 'necessitated by circumstances'. The Board was in what in Physics is described as a state of 'unstable equilibrium', split between pro-regime loyalists fearful of upsetting the status quo, and an enlightened lobby pressing for a shake-up. My diary noted: "If and when the present leadership topples there will be a lot of pieces to be picked up by whoever takes over". Little did I then know that the person was going to be me!

Hard act to follow?

In May 1997 1 took over from Mrs Lin Williams for 9 months as Head

FAST-TRACK PROMOTION (VERY FAST!).

On 1st May I wrote in my letter home to family and friends in UK: "Things may come to a crunch this week-end. It is hard to see any way out than a radical re-shuffle of the top positions". How right I was! I noted that there were rumblings from disenchanted parents, the Board of Governors was mostly confused and dithering, the staff split between diehard supporters of the Headmistress, a somewhat bewildered 'wait and see' majority, and a 'reform lobby' which included me. On top of all this 600 pupils were due to burst onto the scene next Tuesday, 6th May, for the start of term.

On that eventful day the Board stopped dithering. At a meeting that evening they voted out of office their pro-Headmistress Chairman, and voted in a heavyweight, a volatile no-nonsense 15-stone Italian. At 9 p.m. I was at home, in pyjamas ready for bed, when a staff colleague knocked on our door. "Michael, the Board of Governors wants to see you – immediately. It's an urgent matter that can't wait, they say". So, round I went – it was nearly 10 p.m. The Chairman came straight to the point. "We have just sent the Headmistress on leave, while various investigations are carried out. Will you please take over the running of the school at 7 a.m. tomorrow morning. You will be Caretaker Head for the time being. Thank you very much".

Next morning came. There was a tense period of interregnum between 7 and 11 a.m. while the deposed Headmistress packed up and left. Then at break in the staffroom I greeted my colleagues with the news that I was their new boss. There was, as my Diary noted, "a ripple of applause, reflecting the majority mood". The diehard loyalists were however "shocked and dismayed", so much so that two of them instantly resigned. Another knee-jerk reaction came from the Deputy Head. He stormed out of the room and then back in again, thrusting two diskettes (Timetable) into my hand and telling me to "b*****well get on with it". Remarkably, he later cooled down and co-operated. (Perhaps not so remarkable;

he had a nice house with a pool, and intended to invite into it a glamorous newly-arrived Mod Languages teacher).

Waiting for me on the Head's desk that Wednesday morning was an ultimatum from the Inland Revenue (ZRA). As the press cutting from the Times of Zambia relates, they had discovered anomalies in PAYE returns from Lechwe over 5 years. The arrears amounted to K.235 *million*. The deadline for compliance was 48 hours away – noon on Friday. If not paid by then, the amount due would *double*. No wonder that the parents of children in "the elite Lechwe School" were described in the newspaper as being "enraged" when this came to light at their PTA meeting.

The only way out of the financial crisis was a bail-out (short-term loan). The Manager at Barclays in Kitwe was sympathetic, but of course asked what security we could offer for the large amount we needed. We rummaged around, found the title deeds for the property and handed them over – i.e. we mortgaged the school to the bank. That enabled us to get off the hook with ZRA, by paying an instalment of the arrears of PAYE owed to them. These had accumulated over 5 years to 237 *million* kwacha! Thereby we avoided the horrendous penalty for non-compliance. Big sigh of relief! Meanwhile the auditors were digging into the school's financial records, resulting in a 21-page report detailing all sorts of 'irregularities'. Mrs Williams saw the writing on the wall, and within a fortnight submitted her resignation. That meant that I went up one notch in seniority, from 'Caretaker' Head to Acting Headmaster. A year later my successor, when writing a testimonial for me and referring to this period, kindly said "He used his skills and experience to put the school on an even keel again. His task was immense and extremely stressful. It is a tribute to him that the school survived".

Early in June there occurred what I described in my diary as 'a day of tragedy'. One of our British pre-University GAP year students was accompanying our Grade 9 on a geography Field Studies trip to North Province, in a 3-vehicle convoy. When one of the drivers got out for a drink at a filling-station, Cecily insisted on taking a turn at the wheel. Travelling dangerously fast on a straight smooth stretch of tarmac, she drove into a wicked pothole. Both left-hand tyres burst, the van rolled over and over, ending up off the road in the bush 100m further ahead. She was killed outright. I had to break the news, by telephone, to her father who was the British Ambassador in Damascus. In her memory her parents set up a charity – Cecily's fund – which enables AIDs orphans in Zambia to enrol at school (which otherwise they would be unable to do).

Cecily's Fund

EDUCATING ZAMBIAN CHILDREN
ORPHANED BY AIDS
www.cecilysfund.com

Cecily's Fund was set up in 1998 in memory of Cecily Eastwood who was volunteering with orphans and teaching in Zambia on her gap year in 1997. She tragically died in a car accident.

It began as a family charity at the Eastwood kitchen table and has since "grown like topsy". It now has 4,500 supporters all over the world and sister organisations in Switzerland and the USA who make it possible for over 9,500 children to go to school. All with a staff of just six people.

Cecily on holiday in Scotland

Cecily's Fund is a non-governmental organisation committed to helping Zambian orphans and vulnerable children to become self-reliant and live healthy and fulfilling lives.

We do this by building relationships with trusted Zambian partner organisations and by working with them to ensure that these children gain knowledge, life skills and HIV information through education.

IN MEMORY OF
CECILY EASTWOOD
"LADY IN RED"
d. 2.6.1997

2

One advantage of my promotion to Headmaster was that I could hand over the duties of Boarding Master. But there was a hiccup. The school Administrator didn't get Alex Jameson's employment permit ahead of his entry into the country. The Immigration Department don't like that (fair enough), insisting that he should exit Zambia before being allowed in again with proper documentation. We sorted it out, and eventually Sylvia and I were able to move just across the road from the Boys Hostel to a new home. "And very nice it is." I said in my Newsletter home. "Plenty of good borehole water, large cool rooms, shady veranda, lovely garden". And of course, without having to be in charge of 24 junior boys night and day. Stress levels went down appreciably, even though I was 'still working at least 12 hours a day under great pressure'.

To all teaching and other staff, Lechwe School   10 December 1997

As you all know, the period for which I was appointed Acting Head ends on 31st December 1997. I could have applied to be confirmed as Head from 1st January 1998 onwards, and quite a number of you kindly encouraged me to do so. But I decided not to let my name go forward for the post of Head. Instead, I will be going back to the classroom as Head of the Modern Languages Department, and will teach German and Economics for the last two terms of my contract.

I 'held the fort' as Acting head at Lechwe for 8 months until the end of 1997, by which time I had had enough of many curious goings-on at Board of Management level. I opted not to apply for the post of Principal. Instead I stepped down, just to be the Head of Department, Modern Languages, in which capacity I served out the remainder of my contract. The tea chests in my shed in the garden remind me of how we packed up our things, flew home, and re-settled in our home in Norfolk in the late summer of 1998.

Hill House, Stody, (Formerly the Three Horse Shoes pub)

Hill House garden

SURPRISE!

You would have thought that my adventures as a Headmaster in Africa had already ended. But No – surprise, surprise! 3 years later B.E.S.O contacted me again. (I say 'again', because I had already done two short-term assignments in Africa with them). This time the need was twofold. Firstly for a Marketing Manager – "We need the school to be known broadly within the country...and to establish the best way to get the appropriate pupils". Secondly "We want to establish the best mode of Administration relevant to the project". In other words the skills of a Head Teacher.

The project was ambitious. "It is planned to start a Primary School (English Medium). The ultimate objective is 400 pupils at all levels (i.e. including secondary)". The driving force was an enterprising businessman, Mr Robert Naibala, wanting to cash in on the boom in fee-paying private education of high quality in Tanzania at that time. 'Mr Robert', as he was known, needed to project the Usa River Academy's image to upper/middle class parents in Arusha District.

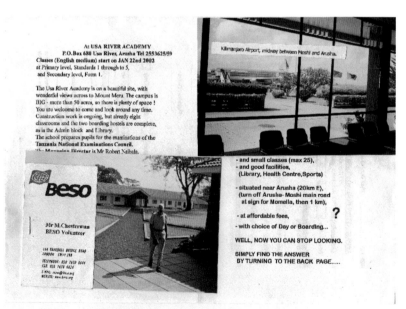

At Kilimanjaro Airport Mr Robert greeted me warmly, but with bad news. "I am sorry to tell you that the Head Teacher is in hospital, seriously ill". Next day she died. So there was no 'counterpart' for me to train. I found myself being Headmaster – again!

Back in Tanzania after 38 years

THE ARUSHA TIMES, OCTOBER 13 - 19TH, 2001

BY A CORRESPONDENT

Last week saw the arrival in Arusha of Michael Chesterman, a retired teacher from England.

He first came to Tanzania in 1962, as the headmaster of a new secondary school being built by the Lutheran church at Magamba, in the Usambara mountains, near Lushoto.

"It was an exciting time," he remembers, "We had a wonderful site on what was previously a golf course. Behind the central classroom block, huge eucalyptus trees towered up into the sky. Once a week all the boys (in Form I and Form II at that time) lined up in their smart school uniforms for a military style parade. They stood to attention, and then the school captain, Mattayo, would march up to the flagpole, halt, and say to me. 'School all present and ready for inspection, sir.'"

"I shall never forget the farewell parade in 1963," continued Chesterman, "My wife and I were walking down the tree-lined avenue, with rows of pupils on each side, when suddenly and without warning there was an earth tremor. The ground shook, and the boys cried out, 'God is angry because you are leaving us.'"

Chesterman recalls how hard the boys studied, like Kuppa and Erasto, who won a science prize for research about different times taken by water to boil. He remembers the encouragement and support given by the Education Secretary of the Lutheran Church.

Rafael Shempemba, and the official opening of the school in February 1963 by the Minister of Education, S. Eliufoo.

What has now brought Chesterman back to Tanzania, at the age of 69?

The answer is that he responded to a request for assistance sent to British Executive Services Overseas (BESO) by an Arusha businessman, Robert Naibala. Naibala is in the process of establishing the Usa River Academy, a new privately-managed primary and secondary school. As a BESO Volunteer Adviser, Chesterman is helping to get the new school up and running - just like Magamba all over again!

Chesterman is happy to lend his expertise to recruiting teaching staff, including a head teacher, overseeing the construction of buildings, purchasing equipment, and enrolling pupils in Standards I - V and Form One.

Parents are welcome to look around the school. It is easy to find, simply turn off the main Arusha-Moshi road at the Momella sign, 20 km east of Arusha. A limited number of places for January 2002 are still available. Tel: 027 2553625/59

Usa River Academy, a new privately-managed primary and secondary school. Michael Chesterman now works as a BESO Volunteer Adviser at the school.

As things turned out, my most useful contribution during my 7 week stay was to recover from Tanzania Revenue Authority 12.5 million shillings (15,000 US dollars) of VAT paid on building materials for the USA River Academy. I attributed this success to 'perseverance and some psychological clout in dealing with obstructive officials'. My report to B.E.S.O ended modestly ... 'In a small way I have helped people out of a hole and added a drop in the bucket of development aid. Every little counts'.

RE: LETTER OF APPRECIATION

We thank you (BESO) for the accompanying us with your volunteer Mr. Michael Chesterman, who for the very short period has been very important for our school.

He really helped us a lot in, advising the teachers and scrutinizing them, the administration of the school and a very useful system for the school to plan in various trips like National park Safaris, Snake parks also advising a good plan of the swimming pool and introduced some games e.g. volleyball and race competition etc.

He also helped us in **TRA** (Tanzania Revenue Authority) whereby we had already surrendered, but Mr. Chesterman came and dealt with them and saved almost **ONE MILLION TSHS** on **VAT**, which is very unexpected.

Due to luck of time we apply for another volunteer if possible we can have Mr. Chesterman back, if not possible any other volunteer for six months from January 2002. This is because our school is still new and we need that support to make sure we are in the right academic track.

We hereby also attach our application form.

RETIREMENT - NOW WHAT?

You have reached the age of retirement. The toils and snares of your career in Africa are behind you. You have resettled in your home in Norfolk. You are in good health. You have four grown-up children and eight grandchildren. What do you do now? Good question. You can't just put your feet up and read the newspaper all day. Fortunately the lawn has to be mowed, the hedges trimmed, autumn leaves swept up, bonfires lit and tended. I find great delight in tending a bonfire, sitting and watching the smoke curl up and away. In the background the sheep graze in the meadow and the stream (beck as we say in Norfolk) trickles down to the Glaven valley a mile away. There is peace and tranquillity, for which my wife and I are grateful and which we enjoy. We harvest our abundance of garden produce, fruit and vegetables, and relax.

The community in which we live, the village of Stody, is small and scattered. Tiny. Only 60 names on the Electoral Register. A large and beautiful church, St Mary's, with a tall round tower. We live next to it, our home having once been the village pub. One avenue of service open to me was to train to be a Lay Reader. In the Church of England vicars are in short supply. The gaps are partly filled by Lay Readers, who are authorised to take services of worship. I completed the required course of training, and on 15th May 1999 at a service in Norwich Cathedral I received my Licence, and my long blue sash

This initiative lasted for 18 months, until in December 2000 I felt it best to give up. I was unable to come to terms with what I described in my letter of resignation as the 'entrenched traditionalism' of the parishioners. They wanted to stick with their liturgical style of worship. No change.

An avenue of service which turned out more successfully for me was in the sphere of local government. Villages have to have Parish Councils, and Councils needs Clerks. Few people apply for the post of Parish Clerk. The job is part-time, tedious, not well paid. Before long I found myself being Parish Clerk, five times over, in local villages! There are heated arguments and disputes about parking on the village green, about gravel pits, about affordable housing being imposed, for reasons of political correctness, by the District Council despite opposition from aggrieved local residents. Redundant red telephone boxes in the village – keep them (for £1), or let them be taken away? Sometimes I didn't know whether I wanted to laugh or cry about parish pump affairs. Wind turbines – are they a 'blot on the landscape' or a good thing – 'clean energy'? Eventually I resigned from all Parish Clerk duties. Time to get back to the bonfire!

PANORAMIC WINDOWS

Panoramic windows.

In August 1999 a surprising new entry appeared on my c.v. Tour Manager !
Anyone browsing through a Sterling River Cruises brochure at that time would
have read about "Your floating hotel, Lady Anne. You will stay on our specially
chartered 3 star vessel, the Lady Anne, in a comfortable cabin with private
facilities. The vessel has four decks, a restaurant, friendly lounge and bar, with
panoramic windows, a sundeck, and a stairlift between all decks".

Included in the deal was the services of a tour manager – a seasonal job for
which I had applied – successfully as it turned out. A chance to view the Rhine
through panoramic windows, and to be paid for doing so, was too good to miss !

Majestic castles tower over the craggy vine clad slopes to the emerald waters of the rivers.
This fabulous cruise is one not to be missed. Relax in the comfort of your friendly cruise vessel as you gently meander through these famous waters. Every view is a picture postcard!

Captain Eelco van Velzen enjoys the trips as much as the two Tour Managers.

Running commentary is needed – not just the geography, but the legends, with Wagner 'Ring' music on tape -Siegfried killing the dragon etc.

Then in 2000 (see below) another opportunity arose – in <u>Austria.</u> Two weeks of healthy outdoors activity, leading guided walks and cycling trips up (in the cable-cars) and then down hills and valleys in <u>Gerlos.</u>

Dear Michael

Welcome to MasterSun Resort Teams 2000! We are pleased to have you working as the MasterSun Rep. in Hotel Glockenstuhl, Austria. Your address in resort will be: Hotel Glockenstuhl, Haus Nr. 250, 6281 Gerlos, Tirol, Austria. Tel: 0043 5284 5217,

JOB DESCRIPTION - *Resort Representative*
Oberammergau Programme - based in AUSTRIA

PURPOSE OF THE POST - Summary

As the only MasterSun staff member based in the resort the Representative plays a key role. It will be his/her task to ensure that all the practical details of the holiday run smoothly for guests, and that the operation is successful.

MAGAMBA RE-BORN

Strange things happen. In this book, a previous chapter entitled 'Magamba' relates how in 1963 my wife and I made an abrupt and dramatic departure from Tanzania. In case you've forgotten, or perhaps skipped over that bit, we were declared to be 'prohibited immigrants'. We had to drop everything and return to UK. My American missionary colleague Paul Gustafson took over from me responsibility as Headmaster of the Secondary School at Magamba. So that chapter closed, and life moved on.

Fast forward 46 years to March 2007. Out of the blue I received astonishing news from Paul. We had kept in touch from time to time through exchange of Christmas Newsletters. The latest of these described how Paul had been in a head-on car crash and had just managed to survive, but with severe injuries. Now came the big surprise. Magamba Secondary School was going to be re-born! Up-graded to the status of a University College, a constituent part of the Lutheran Tumaini University, Tanzania. Magamba would become SEKUCo, the Simon Kolowa University College. The Official Opening and Dedication Ceremony would be in October. We were invited to attend!

It can be a mistake to go back and re-visit after many years the scene of former labours. Post-colonial Africa and independence was not all progress. Many institutions went downhill into neglect or abandonment. Railways, airlines, universities – many of them struggled to keep going. But here was a success story, with substantial backing from international donors. Sylvia and I accepted the invitation, packed our bags, got our jabs, and flew out to Kilimanjaro Airport.

Overnight at the Lutheran Hostel in Moshi, then a long (4 hours+) tedious drive by coach to the turn-off at Mombo. There to meet us was a former (1961) Magamba student of ours – Salatiel Shemhilu. Now a senior official in the Usambara-Digo Lutheran Church he drove us up the steep escarpment into familiar territory – the eucalyptus forest area around Lushoto.

Now came one of the happiest days in our life. At the Dedication Ceremony we were treated like VIPs, seated alongside the Prime Minister. Lots of top brass, two brass bands, choirs. Robed pastors and bishops in solemn procession. Full-throated singing of "Mungu wetu ndiye Boma" (Ein feste Burg) – a flashback to the Opening Ceremony held at Magamba Secondary School on 9 Feb 1963. With tears of joy in our eyes we managed a short greeting in our best Swahili, to top up the other speeches. All very nostalgic, but why not? You could say that the wheel had turned full circle.

Three Bishops and the Prime Minister of Tanzania at Magamba 2007

Did you know that Magamba is now going to be a University !
Can you believe it ? Yes, it is true – Simon Kulowa University.
The Secondary School has closed - Government policy, for
reasons which I don't know. But the ELCT remained the owner
of the land and buildings, and Magamba will be re-born as
SEKUCo. There will be two campuses, Campus A where the
Trade School was, and Campus B on the Secondary School site.

Subj:	**Yes, you are welcome!!**
Date:	15/03/07 10:56:02 GMT Standard Time
From:	*annethmunga@elct-ned.org (Anneth Munga)*
To:	*Pamodzi@aol.com*

Dear Mwl. and Mama Chestermann,

AMANI IKAE NANYI!!   *(Peace be with you!)*

With this email I want to inform you that:
1. I have already informed the Management Team of the headoffice that you
as well as the Gustafsons are planning to attend the Dedication Ceremony
of SEKUCo in October.
2. The dates you mentioned are OK. However, I will have to check with our
Gen. Secretary whether it is possible to arrange transport for you from KIA.

Regarding the dedication:
IT WILL TAKE PLACE IN THE ASSEMBLY HALL AT CAMPUS B I.E.
FORMER
MAGAMBA SECONDARY SCHOOL. WE WILL HAVE MANY CHOIRS

LUNCH WILL BE SERVED AND THAT WILL END THE CELEBRATION. WITH
THE
EXPERIENCE FROM OTHER SERVICES OF THIS KIND, THE SERVICE WILL
TAKE
AT LEAST 4 HOURS!!

Front-row VIP status
for Paul Gustafson,
myself and Sylvia....

and a cordial handshake
with the former President
of Tanzania and First Lady.

Short speech...
"Ni furaha sana
(I am very happy)
kuwa hapa leo".
(to be here today).

The Prime Minister (L), Rt Hon Edward Lowassa, is escorted by the University Chancellor.

WAHUSIKA KWA MATUKIO MAALUM

Kiongozi wa Ibada	Mha. Dr. Stephen Ismail Munga	Askofu KKKT – DKMS *Bishop*
Wasaidizi	Mch. Jonathan Mwamboza	Dean, KKKT – DKMS
	Mha. Ask. Mst. Joseph Jali	Askofu Mstaafu KKKT DKMS *Bishop*
Guest of Honour **Mgeni Rasmi** *Prime Minister, Republic of Tanzania*	Mhe. Edward Lowassa	Waziri Mkuu, Jamhuri ya Muungano wa Tanzania
Mhubiri	Mch. Seppo Rissanen	Mkurugenzi wa - FELM
Msimamizi wa Utaratibu – Ufunguzi	Mch. Dr. Anneth Munga	Mkuu wa Chuo cha *Provost* Sebastian Kolowa
Salaam za Chuo Kikuu cha Tumaini *Chancellor of Tumaini University*	Prof. John Shao	Makamu Mkuu wa Chuo Kikuu cha Tumaini (TU)
Matangazo na Utambulisho	Bw. Salatiel Shemhilu	Katibu Mkuu, DKMS *Chief Exec*
	Mhe. Mohamed Abdulaziz	Mkuu wa Mkoa – Tanga
Mpiga Kinanda *former (1961) pupil Form I at Magamba Sec. Sch.*	Bw. Grayson Hermas	Mwalimu wa Muziki Usharika wa Kisosora – Tanga

Salatiel Shemhilu (L), now Chief Executive of the Lutheran Church, was a former pupil of mine in Form 1 at Magamba Secondary School in 1961 (46 years previously !).

A FAMILY TO BE PROUD OF

Arise, Sir Clement!

The picture (outside Buckingham Palace) is all smiles, and deservedly so.

In 1974 my father Dr Clement Chesterman was knighted, for his services to tropical medicine. Accompanying him was my mother Lady Winifred, my elder brother David, and my sister Hazel (born at Yakusu in the Belgian Congo).

As a knight Sir Clement was entitled to a Coat of Arms. I indirectly benefit from this, as the Arms and Crest 'may be borne and used by him and his descendants' with due and proper differences, according to the Laws of Arms'.

The Coat of Arms needed some explaining...

'The red cross alludes to your medical career

The tsetse flies and syringe commemorate your life's work in the eradication of disease.

The crossbow comes from the arms of your Wunderlich and de Merveilleux ancestors. The Motto is your own ingenious suggestion.'

NON ARCU SED ACU is a snappy pun in Latin. It means 'Not by the bow but by the needle'.

Clever, eh? If ever I get round to doing my own crest 'with due and proper differences' I will be hard pressed to match this one!

The wording of the document is quaint –

'TO ALL AND SINGULAR to whom these Presents shall come Sir Anthony Richard Wagner KCVO Principal King of Arms, sends greeting...Whereas Sir Clement Clapton Chesterman, KnightOfficer of the most excellent Order of the British Empire, FRCP ...did represent to the most noble Duke of Norfolk Earl Marshal of England...that he is desirous of having Armorial Bearings duly assigned... KNOW YE THEREFORE that We do by these Presents grant and assign to the said Sir Clement Clapton Chesterman the arms following...'

Psalm 127 v.5 says 'Happy is the man who has his quiver full of them' (children). Well, here is the quiverful with which my wife Sylvia and I have been blessed.

Our present family. Sylvia's birthday 2010

Read from R to L in the back row:

Our eldest son Graham is a long-serving P.E. teacher. He rose to the rank of Head of Department but nowadays is called Director of Sport.

Next to him are Ian and his wife Mandy. Ian specialised in Agriculture and has spent all his working life in Africa - Zambia, Kenya (twice), Zimbabwe and Ethiopia. As a manager he ran big food-producing estates, then moved into consultancy, controlling big development projects for training African farmers.

Next comes our daughter Sue, with her partner Haydn. Sue's job is what used to be called Personnel Manager but is now renamed HR (Human Resources).

Then there is our 3rd son Colin, with Wendy. Colin was born in Ghana, so he also has African names - Kofi, Mensa, meaning 3rd son, born on a Friday.

Our four children have between them produced 8 grandchildren, so it's all smiles in the front row.

Dear Reader,

It wasn't all plain sailing but thanks for coming along with me for the ride. I hope you enjoyed it.

Goodbye!

Printed in Great Britain
by Amazon.co.uk, Ltd.,
Marston Gate.